Techniques of
Motor Cycle
Road Racing

FOREWORD

'I am a motor cycle racer, not a writer. To get
this book done, I had to work with someone
who not only writes but understands motor
cycle racing. Peter Clifford has been Editor of
Motocourse pretty well since I came into
Grand Prix racing. I can't think of anybody
better qualified to work with me – at least he
knew what I was talking about.'

Kenny Roberts

Techniques of
Motor Cycle
Road Racing

Kenny Roberts

Edited by Peter Clifford

Hazleton Publishing, Richmond, Surrey

PUBLISHER
Richard Poulter

EXECUTIVE PUBLISHER
Elizabeth Le Breton

ART EDITOR
Steve Small

PRODUCTION CONTROLLER
Peter Lovering

This first edition published in 1988 by Hazleton Publishing, 3 Richmond Hill,
Richmond, Surrey TW 10 6RE.
ISBN: 0 905 138-51-1
Printed by Butler and Tanner Ltd, Frome, Somerset.
Typesetting by First Impression Type Ltd, Richmond, Surrey.

Cover photographs by David Goldman and Takanao Tsubouchi.

Colour photography by:

Malcolm Bryan	– pages 132-133, 142(left), 144(top)
David Dewhurst	– page 144(bottom)
Takanao Tsubouchi	– pages 129, 130-131, 134, 135, 136-137, 138-139, 140-141, 142-143

Black and white photography by:

Allsport, Tom Beesley, T.J.M. Beijerbacht, Malcolm Bryan, Paul-Henri Cahier, W.P. Castricum,
Champion, Rich Chenet, Peter Clifford, David Dewhurst, Mush Emmons, Richard Francis, Jan
Hesse, Brian Kelly, Henk Keulemans, Charles B. Knight, LAT, Marlboro World Championship
Team, Manfred Mothes, Kent Peterson, Pietro Sanna, Leo Vogelzang, Ron Whitby, Mick Woollett.

Acknowledgements:

Peter Clifford wishes to thank Louise, Dean Miller, Peter Ingley and Mike Sinclair.

DISTRIBUTORS

UK & OTHER MARKETS, **Osprey Publishing Limited,**
12-14 Long Acre, London WC2E 9LP

USA, **Motorbooks International,** PO Box 2, 729 Prospect
Ave., Osceola, Wisconsin 54020

AUSTRALIA, **Technical Book & Magazine Co. Pty,**
289-299 Swanston Street, Melbourne, Victoria 3000

NEW ZEALAND, **David Bateman Ltd,** PO Box 65062,
Mairangi Bay, Auckland 10

CONTENTS

INTRODUCTION

When I started racing I just took my 250 Ducati road bike and went charging round and round Snetterton on a Sunday afternoon. Sometimes I crashed, very occasionally I won, but I always had a great time. I got faster, graduated to a TD3 Yamaha and was more successful so I thought I was doing just fine. In fact, I was digging myself into a hole. As I tried to progress from club to national level and home internationals I quickly found that I lacked the ability or the knowledge to compete.

I assumed that I lacked ability and nothing I have learned since has changed my mind on that score. Very few racers have the natural skill to be national title-holders, far less World Champions, but if I knew then what I know now I would have been far better qualified to judge what was a shortcoming in my knowledge and experience and what a lack of natural ability. If I had been able to listen to Kenny Roberts when I started racing I would have benefited from his experience and thus would probably have crashed less frequently and certainly been able to make better use of whatever talent I had.

It is probably too late for me to be World Champion, but I am now putting Roberts's words of wisdom to good use and I can see where they make practical sense out on the track. Never mind that an amateur like me can make use of the great man's expertise – Kenny Roberts's verdict on a line, a corner, a bike, a rider, a tyre, anything concerned with racing motor cycles is sought by every top Grand Prix rider. After all, they still call him 'King Kenny'.

Roberts often illustrates his points with stories from his own experiences, so this book is as much autobiographical as it is instructional. It was written mostly at his home in California, where many great riders come to train, ride dirt bikes, measure themselves against the master and no doubt take note of what he has to say. This is a book of his words and as such I believe anyone who is interested in racing motor cycles, from the raw beginner to the professional, has something to learn from it.

Kenny Roberts was never foolish enough to believe that he knew everything there was to know about racing and hence there are major contributions from Peter Ingley, Dean Miller and Mike Sinclair, experts he relies on for their specialist knowledge. From the start of the book Roberts makes no secret of how he used experts he trusted, from his earliest mentor, Bill Robinson, and then Kel Carruthers, who helped him to become the best road racer in America, and then triple World Champion.

It is quite obvious from listening to Roberts that the technical ability to ride fast round corners is only half the story. You have to be impressed with the guy's determination, the irrepressible drive to be the best and always give 100 per cent. I know that Kenny Roberts feels that giving everything is a prerequisite of success. If you are prepared to do that then there are few limits to what you might achieve.

Peter Clifford

Chapter 1

World Champion

I probably worked at racing more than anyone else. Everything else was second to being a road racer. I just worked more hours at it and it paid off.

The motivation to win and to keep going when things seem to be against you is all-important. It is not always easy to see where that comes from. In my case I think it came from the way I was raised – it was different from most kids. From the age of ten I just about raised myself and I was a mean S.O.B. I started racing motor cycles when I was fourteen and all I cared about was winning. That was all I cared about with anything I did at that time, and it has been the same ever since. It's like that with most racers. It is only just recently that I have started to get a bit more mellow: I don't always have to win every golf game or whatever.

But no matter how determined you are, you can't do everything alone. You have to have people around you whom you can trust, who are there for you. I had a good friend in Bill Robinson. He helped me so much when I started racing. If I screwed up he let me know it, but he was always there to help out when it was needed. Bud Aksland was like a father at times. We had some real blow-outs, fights just like a father and son can have, but we always got together again afterwards and had a lot of respect for each other.

If you are going to expect help from people – and they will be doing it because they want to see you succeed – then you must put in 100 per cent effort. It's no good doing anything at 90 per cent because you won't fool them and you will only be fooling yourself.

Kel Carruthers always worked his heart out: the guy would take the cranks out half an hour before the race if that is what he had to do to win it. And I always rode at 100 per cent. Like Kel has said in the past: 'We work hard and if the rider doesn't work 100 per cent we lose our enthusiasm.' If the team loses their enthusiasm for the rider, everything just goes flat and falls down.

There were years when the guys did lose their enthusiasm for both me and the equipment because we were not getting the results, but we were able to salvage something. We could talk about it, discuss the problems together and pull something out of the mess. It would really help if the rider could be more of a manager at times – or at least learn how to deal with people. The best thing that could happen to some of the guys is to run a small team, so they would have to learn what it takes to get the best from people. A rider gets a very small, narrow, thin view of life. He has to have it to a certain extent, but he also needs someone like Kel who can say, 'Hang on, you can't act like that. You can't just fly off home because things are not going too well – you have got to go testing.' The rider probably feels that the last thing he wants to do at that point is go testing, but for himself and the morale of the rest of the team he has to buckle down and get on with sorting out the problem. The team comes first: this is your job and if you are a professional you are going to do it right. There may be a lot of bitching, screaming and yelling at times, but the work has to get done. On the other hand, the rider has to have some time off to relax. It's getting harder and harder, with fifteen or sixteen Grands Prix and all the testing that needs to be done, and that is why someone who understands all this has to manage the team. Someone has to get the priorities right.

If I said I didn't want to test, and the factory said OK, then I would know that when I came in after practice at the next race and told them that the bike was no good they could quite rightly look me straight in the eye and say, 'Hey, you're the one that didn't want to test. You're the one who couldn't spare the time, so don't bitch about the tyres, the engine or the suspension.'

That was the decision I had to face when I decided to retire. I wanted to spend more time with the family and I was not prepared just to fly to races on Thursday and get on the bike, like Freddie did. I was not prepared to do that. I was either going to do all the testing and preparation that was needed, or I was going to retire. When I was racing I once flew from home to England to test tyres for two hours, then flew home again. It got to the point where I wasn't prepared to do that any more, and that is one of the reasons I stopped.

It's a tough life, but Wayne Gardner comes over to Europe for the duration of the season. You don't see him flying home at every opportunity. Randy had to do that when he rode for me in '87. I said he had to have a home in England because I know what it is like – with jet lag from flying about all over the place you are useless for days. It has to take the edge off your performance.

It is possible to win the World Championship without being the best rider in the world. On the other hand, if you look back through the records, there are those who were very special, who could win on whatever bike they were given even if it was not as good as the opposition. To me riders like Dick Mann and Cal Rayborn were like that in road racing, and Mert Lawill on the dirt. They could ride no matter what – like Kel, he had a private bike a lot of the time during his years in the World Championships. He just rode the best that he could. He knew it would do no good to pout and say, 'Well I don't have a works bike' – he had to ride it in the end.

The guys I rode against, like Lucchinelli and Uncini, were very serious and determined about what they were doing and they won the World Championship. There are others who just miss out on winning because they are not so determined and dedicated. I think that Gregg Hansford was one of those. He had such a lot of ability but he didn't really have the drive or the pure dedication it took to win the World Championship.

When he did have it, he didn't have the equipment to do the job. It is easy to be critical of such people, but just because Gregg Hansford didn't eat and sleep motor cycles like I did does not make him any less of a rider, or less of a person. Everyone is human, when all is said and done, and even though I was trying to beat them I still respected all of them.

Uncini won the World Championship and he was one of the most professional racers I have ever met. Just talking to Franco and getting his views on racing was an education. He is very smart and knows so much about racing he is able to weigh up both sides and point out the good and the bad in so many areas of the sport.

Racing does bring out the very cream of the crop. The leading riders didn't get to the top on luck and they aren't stupid. When I say things that sound over-critical it's because I'm a member of this special circle and I am judging others by the highest possible standards. The difference between these guys is real small because they are all great riders. It was not just me and Barry Sheene riding around, or me and Freddie riding around – there are a lot of other fine riders out there.

Not quite the style of Roberts the World Champion but this is early days (1971), before it occurred to Kenny to move his weight away from the centre line. Kel Carruthers won this combined 250/lightweight race at Daytona while Roberts finished fifteenth.

Determination is one of the things that separates most of the guys from the really great racers. There seem to be a lot of riders, especially in Europe, who think that, because they don't have a works bike, they can never do any good. When Mike Baldwin went to his first GP in Spain in 1979 he set fastest time on a private Suzuki. The works bikes were behind. He had his bike, and he rode the hell out of it, and he got third at the end of the day after a bad start. Few riders can do that.

Freddie Spencer has more natural talent than just about anyone else I have ever seen, and he combines that with real aggression, an almost ruthless will to win. I don't know what happened to him after '85 — why he was not competitive through '87 — but it has to be in his head. 1983 took a lot out of him. We were both racing flat out every week. We never talked about it but I always thought that who won each race was not as important as being the fastest guy on the race track that day. The two aren't always the same thing. I thought that I was the fastest man out there but I guess he might think differently.

Being fastest man on the track that year was not quite enough to win the Championship, even if that's what gives you the greatest satisfaction. There is so much that goes into winning the Championship – your natural ability, the talent you develop, experience, luck, the machine, reliability, tyres and the opposition. If you are going to be World Champion all these things have to come together. But to succeed at all you have to be better than the other guy, and no matter what natural ability you have, you will have to work at it. The guys who ask, 'What do I have to do to be Champion?', who mean it and will follow it through, are the ones who will get there.

I used to think a lot during the close season about how I could be more prepared for the year ahead, what I had to do to get myself into a condition to win. That was all that mattered to me, who my opponents were going to be, what I would have to do to beat them, what they were good at. If I had raced them before I would have a fair idea how they rode a motor cycle and what their strong points were.

The bike is important as well, and I always had a good idea in what area their bike was better if I had raced against it before. Then the hard part was to get Yamaha to improve our bike, to where we could beat it. Of course you never know what the opposition is going to have for the coming season, but it is a pretty good guess that it will be better than they had last year and that they will be working on the areas where your bike might have been better the season before.

All in all I used to think about the opposition — what lines they used, what race tracks they went best at, what times during the race or the season they went fast and when they didn't — and try to figure out the reasons behind all of that. Things change all through the year but you work at it during the winter. It is all part of self-motivation, keeping your mind on training and why you are doing things. You are training to beat someone even when you are exercising, running, or riding a motocross bike on your own: the idea at the end of it is to beat the other guy, even though he isn't there.

Take the year before Freddie came Grand Prix racing. I knew Freddie's riding style because I had raced him in the States. He used the front to the limit, which I did not have to do at that particular time. I could ease up on the front so I was very light on front tyres and hard on rear tyres. But by the end of the following season I was harder on front tyres than anybody. I trained towards that point. I knew that if I was going to use the front tyre harder, push it to the limit, I was going to have to be in better condition. If you push things closer to the limit at any time you need to be in top physical condition. If you are not, you run out of concentration and you will run off the track.

In the year that Freddie and I went at it together that was our problem, we were using our mental capacity so much that we were exhausted. That is why he ended up pushing us both off the track in Sweden. We had both been under so much mental pressure that in the end he just blew a fuse. He told me that it took a whole year out of him: he said the next season he just couldn't do it. I retired so I didn't have to come back and do it again, but it sure took a lot out of me as well.

If you are going to win the World Championship what you have to do is to look at the opposition and say: 'What do I have to do to beat those guys?' I think that is what's lacking at the moment, there are too few people prepared to do it. I think that Eddie looks at racing like this. Randy didn't, but he should now, because while he was riding for my team we taught him to think about what he had to do to win. There are too few people who do that.

Take 1983. I knew Freddie was going to be a big threat. He was a young kid with an enormous amount of talent, fresh onto the scene like a lion. He had never won the World Championship so he had everything to gain. I had to prepare myself mentally and physically for that. It takes a lot of discipline. Instead of playing golf you have to be out training. Instead of running two miles you have to run four. You have to decide what it is that is stopping you from going faster. Is it your strength? Can you figure out what it is that limits your lap speed?

Some guys just race and are happy to say, 'Well, I got fifth', or 'I got second'. Others are different. When I first met Gardner he was little more than a kid, maybe eighteen. He was travelling with Jeff Sayle and had gone to Assen to see what a Grand Prix was all about. We all went to Amsterdam one night, between there and the Belgian Grand Prix, and that's when I met him for the first time. They told me he'd raced in Australia but I didn't know him from Adam. He talked to me quite a bit and he said, 'I want to be World Champion one day' – and I guess he meant it. Those are the kids that are dangerous, the ones who go to a race and say, 'What do I have to do to win at that?'

It is the same with a young guy like John Kocinski. Working with him is a relief because all he wants is to be the best. If I said, 'Hey John, when you get up in the morning you have got to do twenty push-ups before you go to the can,' he would do it. Not that I would tell him to do it, but if that's what it took he would do it. At the other extreme, you might be working with someone, trying to get them to do what you want, when they are not really interested. There are a lot of riders who just don't have the desire to win, they don't want it badly enough, or they are lazy, or just don't want to know. They think they are a big star and that everyone around them thinks they are a big star and why should they have to bust their ass working at it. They just want to go out with their wife or girlfriend, drink and have a good time. Going fast does not work like that. Riders might get to a certain point because they have some natural talent, but every year they have to look objectively at their skills, where they can make them better and what they have to do to go faster. Otherwise they are just going to slide off the pace and they will never improve.

I know the way that I used to look at racing. I was serious about it. My way of doing things does not suit everyone, but I believe that if you don't attack the problem seriously there will always be someone else who will, and unless you just have so much more natural talent than he does you will never win.

Of course, there are times when you cannot win because the equipment that you are on is just not up to it. Perhaps the opposition has the better tyres or the better bike, and no matter how hard you try you cannot overcome such disadvantages. Take 1982, when Uncini won the World Championship. He was using Michelin tyres and we had Dunlops. At that time the Dunlop front was not very good; Michelin had a great front tyre that season. Uncini would say to me, 'I can't slide the front, I keep pushing and pushing the front and I can't make it slide.' He had jumped on the works bike and taken advantage of it and the tyres. He was unbeatable strictly because of that. Not taking anything away from him, he was riding harder than he ever rode before. When you look at the whole thing together – the man, the motor cycle and the tyres – it makes a little more sense.

The following year I had a motor cycle I could ride, and I had tyres that lasted the race most of the time. I finally had a bike that I could ride harder and harder and harder, not one that went five laps and then the shock would fade and I'd have to spend the rest of the race trying to hang on to the damn thing, trying to keep it on the race track. I can remember times on the old OW60 when I should have pulled in and parked it, because it was unridable. There were occasions when the factory said we could drop it. But we would have lost face if we had gone back: I wanted to go forward and make a better bike, so I kept riding it. We sacrificed a year with that bike.

When Uncini won the World Championship he was riding better than just about everyone else, and he was making full use of the machine. The next year it wasn't the same. He didn't have the same advantage, because my bike was working well and so were the Hondas. That was the year he had his accident at Assen and was hit by Gardner, who couldn't avoid him. I never saw them collide but you have to put it out of your mind. It's funny, but I was never one to be affected by that sort of thing. Even when I saw that some guy had crashed and thought, hell he must be hurt crashing there, it didn't affect my performance. I used to think that there was something wrong with me because nothing could affect the way I rode. I had the attitude that this was my job, I just had to get on with it, and there was nothing I could do to help. I did have to tell myself to get on with riding or I might end up doing the same thing. I used to say, 'You stupid son of a b...., why do it there?' – more mad at him for making a mistake than anything else.

Things do get to you though. I have had friends get killed, too many, but

Kenny checks the twin-shock suspension while Kel models the latest in corporate headwear. It is 1974, the Ontario 200-miler and the 700 Yamaha is still a beast to be held in awe, wire wheels and all.

I had to stop it affecting my riding. I knew that if I let anything interfere with my concentration while I was out there riding, the same thing could happen to me. I guess we are all the same. I felt that it couldn't happen to me on the one hand, but on the other I knew it could.

You spend a lot of time convincing yourself that you can do anything, that you are super human. But another part of you is telling yourself that you're only human, that you could get hurt. I guess it is a bit of a battle between the two. In the end it is total commitment to your ability and trust in your ability that gets you through. If you have 100 per cent trust in your ability then your brain will not say:'Yes, but you could fall off.'

I also had to keep telling myself not to get too pumped up. That was my problem. I would get so pumped up before going out and I was always battling to control it. I was getting too aggressive, I wanted to go out and murder the opposition.

It did get the better of me a couple of times. Once at Oulton Park, when we were racing in the Match Races in the early years, we'd been told that 'Yanks can't ride in the rain'. It was the last race of the series. We had the competition won, all I had to do was finish the race. I had something like a twenty-second lead and then something clicked in my head, I don't know why. I said to myself, 'I'm going to show these guys that we can ride in the wet.' So I started going faster, and then faster and faster. Coming down the front straight the bike was weaving like the 700s did. As it wobbled it would load and unload the front forks. I happened to nail the front brake with the load off the forks and without weight on the front tyre it just locked up. The bike went down on its side instantly, no time to react. It was pretty stupid and Kel said, 'What the hell did you do that for?' I said, 'I don't know, I wanted to go faster.' I felt inside that I was going to lap everybody, I guess. I was young and stupid. I thought about it and thought about why I did it, but I have always had a battle right through my career.

In '83 I did something pretty stupid at Monza. It had been wet all through practice and we were having trouble with the bikes. There was a problem with the disc valves and we didn't get them altered till the end of practice. We had three wet sessions, then the last one was dry. I was desperate to test the bike because I was determined that I could beat that Honda, if only the engine would run right. When we warmed the bike up for that session I knew we had it sorted and I was ready to go. Eddie was still trying to learn the track and wanted to follow. I said 'Fine', but by the time they let us out onto the track I was pumped. I went round the first half of the track and back under the old banking and, man, I just smoked into that next chicane. Eddie said later, 'Jesus Chr... No way I was going to follow you, no way.' As I braked for the corner I was thinking, 'That's it, the engine is right.' Then I flicked it in and it never even started to turn an inch. It went straight on, but lying right on its side and sliding up the road. It happened so fast I was still riding it on its side as I slid laughing into the gravel pit. I was kicking myself then, because I was so pumped up I had lost my mind. I had been racing for so many years and done so many tyre tests, probably more than anyone in the world, but I had gone out with new tyres and flicked the thing away. Now that's stupid.

That was always my problem, pumping myself up so much that I was disregarding the world and what was going on around me. I tried to view

In the Anglo-American Match Races in 1976, Roberts scored one win, three seconds and a third before falling in the last race at Oulton Park.

racing a bike as a job that I did not have to get pumped up about to be able to do. So I spent a good amount of time pumping myself down, just because when I did get pumped up there was no telling what I might do.

Guys have different ways of pumping themselves up. Some do it with their mouths, telling themselves that they're great, they're awesome, but that never worked for me. One thing that made me confident, pumped up to a point, if you wish, was concentrating on a problem with the motor cycle – so if I got it sorted out I knew I could go faster. Another was knowing that I was in better shape than the rest of the guys, knowing that I could last the race and thinking that they could not. That gave me the confidence I needed. I didn't have to go telling myself I was the best rider in the world or that I was better than everyone else. What would get me going was the technical, the mechanical side of the motor cycle, telling the machine engineers or the tyre engineers what was needed to make the bike faster. If we worked at the bike and made it better, that gave me all the confidence I needed.

Through my riding career I have been fortunate to work with some great tyre engineers. In my early years, riding in the States, there was Bill Robinson, a very good friend of mine who I travelled around with for a few years. Another was John Smith, who worked in Goodyear's engineering department and came to Europe with me in 1978. In '79 Tim Miller became Goodyear's Grand Prix technician, and when I went to Dunlop I started to work with Peter Ingley. I formed a special relationship with these tyre people. It is something that some riders build up, that closeness with the tyre engineers. As Bill Robinson used to say, 'The tyre is the only thing that keeps your ass off the ground.'

I always had faith in those guys, to the point where I would believe completely in what they told me. I remember John Smith once told me that on a wet track with no puddles a slick would work as well as an intermediate, provided that the compound was warm. I believed John Smith with my life, I trusted all of those guys with my life, because they knew more about tyres than I did. I found it great that I could walk into the truck, or they would come to the motorhome, and I could bounce questions off them. I might say, 'I want to go through this corner faster but there is something telling me I can't do it and that something is coming from the rear tyre, maybe it is just collapsing too much.' They would give me some sort of input. Whether it was the 100 per cent correct answer or not did not matter because it was more information to put into my computer that would help me come up with a solution.

I trusted these guys and through my career I had a unique relationship with them and bounced so many ideas off them. 'Why, when I stick the bike into the corner, does it want to stand up?' Obviously that must be a characteristic of the bike if things are not set up correctly, but of all the people in my pit it was always the tyre guy who got the most questions. 'Why can't we get a bigger tyre, why can't we run a smaller tyre, why can't we get a profile that will make the bike flick in quicker or get more traction while I am leaned over?' It's something you can't stress enough, something you have to work on when you are on your way up through racing or just getting to Grand Prix level. *The tyre people know more than you do.* They work with the best so they have that knowledge. I always had a lot of respect for tyre people and the effect they could have on my career, helping me go faster.

The other people, of course, are the engineers I have worked with – Kel, Maekawa. I always picked their brains, asked them what if ..., how come we can't do this or that, make the engine narrower, and why does it have to be that wide because then I could get the engine lower and go round the corner faster. You have to be constantly talking to these people and have a good working relationship with them.

I've always treated the people I work with as equals, because they are equals. When I went Grand Prix racing some of the European riders didn't have that attitude, but it was something Bill Robinson taught me a long, long time ago, that these people are just as important as you are and if you don't treat them right then you are not going to go very far. A rider is not higher up the scale than a tyre engineer or a mechanic. Everyone there has a job to do and they should do it with equal pride. A lot of the riders have egos that have to be massaged, but the mechanics have egos as well. Everyone wants to do the best job that they possibly can and they also want to be congratulated when they do it. They don't like to get stepped on.

The attitude of some riders always puzzled me. It was like that with Sheene: when he won, the bike was OK but he was fantastic; if it wasn't for his riding the bike would not have got anywhere. I remember reading through some of the *Motocourses* in '78, when I went to Europe. Sheene had said in '77 that the Yamaha was a lot faster but he was able to beat Steve Baker because the Suzuki accelerated quite well; or he said that the standard Suzuki was quicker than his on top speed but he could make up for it because of his riding ability and the fact that the factory bike was a little lighter.

The point is that I sometimes won races because my bike was faster than anyone else's. Half my career the bike was faster than I was able to ride it and it is important that the engineers and the mechanics that helped make it good get the recognition, because that is part of what keeps them going. All such relationships are important in racing, even with the less obvious people — the oil guys, the helmet designers all helped me in my career. It is all an exchange of input, of information. There have been times when a rider not in the top twenty at the Grands Prix has made a suggestion to Tim Miller or Peter Ingley that made sense to me, and I used it and went faster.

When things do go wrong in a race you have to understand enough about the motor cycle to know what is amiss and what consequence it will have. One time I was riding a dirt track race in Delaware, New Hampshire. It was a heat and I needed to come third to transfer to the final. I was running mid-pack and then started to run it up high and make some ground. Suddenly the handlebars started shaking and I felt that either the engine was falling out or the crank was going away. I happened to look down, going along the back straight, and saw that the swinging arm pivot bolt was coming out. It was sticking out several inches but instead of pulling over and stopping I kept going: I knew how long the bolt was and I realised that I could keep going. I kicked it back in, and went on doing that on each straight, but because I was rolling the throttle off and on in the corner it would work its way out again. I realised that there was no danger of it coming out altogether while I could keep kicking it back in because, under full power, the motor torque would hold it in place. I went the second half of the race like that and worked my way up to second place.

You could say that riding dirt track doesn't help you, because there are champions who have never ridden on the dirt. You could say riding a mini bike doesn't help, or riding a trials bike either, but when it comes down to it they are all pieces of equipment, all motor cycles that you have to manoeuvre, and the more experience you have on a motor cycle the better you are going to be.

*World Championship
number one: Roberts
crosses the line ahead of
Barry Sheene and
Takazumi Katayama at
the Nürburgring to clinch
the title. He didn't need to
win the race as he led
Sheene, his only
challenger, by eight points
going into the final round.
He thought the
Nürburgring was
dangerous but he
approached it as a
professional, learnt it on
a road bike and broke the
lap record as soon as he
got on the 500 Yamaha in
unofficial practice.*

In road racing you can get into the situation that the front tyre is chattering so badly that you can't lean the bike over. When that happened to me I would just go a lot slower into the corner and square it off harder, using the back more. If the back starts to give up then you have to rely more on the front, adapt your riding, change lines and work around the problem.

There was a time in Italy that the OW61 was handling real bad – the tyre had gone off, the chassis was flexing, the shock had given up and the bike was all over the road. Trying to get it out of the hairpin it was doing a horn dance like a wild steer. I scared Marco Lucchinelli so much that he told Italian TV that he could have beaten me but he knew I was going to crash. He said that there was no way he could stick right behind me because it was bucking and sliding all over the place. Well I knew it was bad, but I also knew that there was no way it was going to throw me off. I ended up coming third so it wasn't one of my better races, but it was probably one of my better rides.

I might have got out of shape a few times riding bikes like the OW61, but that isn't the idea. The idea is to get a bike that works better than the others. I always saw that as my job even if I had to pay to do it, and I did one year: I paid Yamaha $100,000 to build me a better bike. We were negotiating for the '82 season and I had my idea of the raise I was going to get. It was the year that they were going to produce the V. They wanted to bring it to Assen but I said I wanted it sooner, I wanted something better than the square four and I wanted it at the beginning of the year. I didn't want to keep developing the square four, I didn't want to waste any more time on it. A square four was what Suzuki had and I wanted something better. Even if it was not as good to start with I didn't care. I wasn't even supposed to know that they had a V design, but I did and so I told them I would take $100,000 less if they would build it for me. They agreed, but I have no idea whether my offer was any sort of consideration for them because $100,000 is really nothing when it comes to producing a completely new bike. But it made them realise I was serious.

John Kocinski gets his first ride on a 500 during a test session at Laguna Seca in January 1987. 'Working with John is so refreshing. He is so keen he will do whatever it takes.'

Chapter 2

Practice

You can teach anyone to be a road racer. Obviously not everyone is going to be a World Champion because there is such a thing as natural ability and that is very hard to measure. No matter how much natural ability you have, though, you still have to learn to race a motor cycle.

Practice means working on the bike so that you can cut the lap time. The grandstands at Spa are deserted but the concentration in the pits is 100 per cent. The Goodyear technicians look on while Carruthers and Nobby Clark work on the rear wheel.

Randy learnt when he first came to Europe from watching me, from following me round the track. You can learn that way, and it's possible to save yourself a lot of time by having someone to watch and someone to answer your questions. For a young road racer that can be important: it can save you perhaps a year, or even a year and a half. I helped Wayne Rainey and Jim Filice early on, when they started road racing seriously. I would say that Wayne learnt the most from me. He would ring up and ask questions, we would go over things on the phone, problems he was having out on the track.

What practice is all about is getting you and the motor cycle to go as fast as you can possibly go. It needs constant preparation and input, input into your own personal computer, until you are ready and the bike has been sorted out as much as possible in the time available. Then you can put together three or four good fast laps, as fast as you and the machine can possibly go.

It is not hard to do but you have to work at it. I have probably had pole time as often as anybody, and it is a matter of pushing each little thing to the limit, finding out what goes wrong first. For example, on the braking, if I am going for a fast time and the bike is starting to dance around at the rear then that leads me to think that the forks are a little too soft on the last inch and a half of their stroke. So I come into the pits and adjust that, and it allows me to brake just a little bit later and pick up a fraction on the lap time. Then, as I go a little bit faster, something else will come to the surface. Perhaps the back suspension is starting to load itself up too much as I go into the corner a little harder, sagging a bit too much, and that is changing the steering geometry, making the bike lazy to steer. This makes the front end feel insecure and will eventually make the back end come around. So then you come in and try more bump damping, or more pre-load, whichever you prefer, and try again. Then you get back out there and find you can go faster, so you are exerting yet more pressure, and perhaps the front forks are sagging and require more oil or a harder spring. Then you know what to expect, you know it is going to be stiffer and will take more abuse. If it works, and you have made the right adjustments, you will usually come up with a faster time without even thinking about it.

In 1979, pushing the Yamaha to the limit, Roberts took pole position for five of the twelve races and won the Championship from Virginio Ferrari and Barry Sheene.

To sort the bike during practice you should pick out the most important corners, usually the fast ones leading into fast sections, where your speed is going to be most vital. I didn't work on low gear corners at all. I don't waste my time there because it makes so little difference to lap times. The effort is better spent on the fast corners.

The main thing is to get the corners that are going to make the biggest difference to lap times down pat. You can go around the other corners as hard as you like, with everything dragging on the ground, and you will not even pick up a tenth in lap time. But go through a set of fast esses just right, at 100 per cent, and you will pick up half a second.

Freddie's strong point has been that he can go out and do a few laps of practice, then change tyres and get an instant fast lap. I like to work up to it. I did it his way when I was young and less experienced. In my first year in Europe I would learn the race track in four or five laps and by the sixth lap would be doing some reasonably fast times. At the end of my Grand Prix career the V four was so demanding, and required such a precise line, that if someone was in my way through a series of corners or I got off line for whatever reason the fast lap was all over. I had to go from white line to white line to get a good time, and it appeared to me that the three-cylinder Honda was a lot more manoeuvrable. Freddie found that out when he had to ride a four.

What I found was that if I got off line it was no good saying to myself, 'OK, let's lean in a little more', it was already on the limit and would not move. In practice I beat Freddie as often as he beat me in '83. We both got pole position six times. In the races where I finished in front of him I just inched away gradually, and was lapping faster at the end of the race than he was at the beginning. That was the way I felt comfortable, to go faster and faster gradually, when I was mentally ready to push the brake markers back little by little and get on the gas earlier and earlier. Inch by inch I was finding the lines and the limit, and it worked for me both in practising and racing. It didn't win me the World Championship that year, but we did come back from a pretty big deficit at the beginning of the season.

When you are out practising it is no good just circulating round and round, trying to work out what you are doing wrong. There are very few people who can sort everything out while they are actually on the motor cycle. Stop at the pits, get off the machine, and have a think about it for a few seconds while the mechanics are putting in fuel, or whatever. You might have been out there busting your brains to do 1m 30s laps and you know the lap record is 1m 28s. Then you come in wondering what the hell you are going to do to find those two seconds.

Come into the pits and go over and over in your mind what you are doing wrong. You might just be off line coming out of one corner – but on a 500, if that is an important corner, that could be a second a lap or at least half a second. Think about it, get the mechanics to make whatever changes need making, then go out there and, by the second lap, you will find you are into the groove again. If you have thought it out right the times will come down.

You must also be aware of what practice sessions there are and the fact that the rest of the sessions may be wet. I never consciously went out to put in a fast lap every session but if you are pushing the bike hard, learning the track and sorting the bike out, you should naturally be putting in fast

Roberts believes that a rider should put everything into practice. Only by pushing the bike to the limit in practice can one learn how it will perform at racing speed. In 1983, when he clashed head to head with Freddie Spencer, Roberts was on pole six times, Spencer being the fastest qualifier for the other six races. They also shared the twelve race wins.

33

At Sears Point in 1979 Roberts takes time off from his second World Championship year to pull a few wheelies for the fans at home. Such displays are not part of the serious racing process and this is certainly not a skill that needs practising.

times. I did so much tyre testing I was always pushing the bike close to the limit, and there was always a tyre technician there waiting to be told how it was going. There's no point in cruising around, because you never find out a thing that way.

It has always amazed me the number of guys who will only do a couple of laps at a time in practice. They might qualify on the front row, or even on pole, but then go two seconds a lap slower in the race. Then they complain that the tyres were no good – well, they never had enough time to test the tyres to see if they would last. Freddie did that at the Belgian GP in '83, then he had a fit after the race because the back tyre had started to go away. He had put on a soft rear when the Michelin technician told him all along he needed a harder back, but he wanted a big lead off the start so he chose the softer one. I had a Japanese Dunlop that was going to last forever, but I went faster on that at the end of the race than he did on his soft front in the first five laps. He never did more than four laps of practice at a time and did not want to test the other compounds, so how could he blame the tyre company for his problems? It was his fault, but he was slagging them for it.

Chapter 3

Picking a line

*Taking a corner on a racing machine is like play-
ing golf. You are always taught to see the shot and
then hit it. If you can't picture the shot and see
what you are going to do then you will never make
it. The same applies to riding a bike. You have to
be able to see the line you want to follow through
the corner – picture it in your mind, where you
want to brake, and turn, and come out.*

I always liked to walk the track before I went out and rode. The most
important thing about walking the track and picking a line is to fix the
whole thing in your head. Unless you have it firmly laid out in your mind
there is no point in trying to go fast.

You don't always have enough time to go out and do a lot of laps on the
bike. I remember when I first went to England, to ride in the Match Races
at Brands Hatch, there were just two twenty-minute practice sessions. I
went out for the first session and rode round, trying to sort the circuit
out. I could only do just so much while I was out on the bike. There was
so little time. Then, before the next session, I went and sat in the back of
the truck, behind a stack of tyres so that no one could see me, because we
had nowhere private to go. I sat there and just went over and over the
track in my mind until I had the layout fixed and I knew where on the
track I wanted to be all the way round. I knew then what I wanted to do,
so it was just a case of going out there and doing it.

By picturing the track in my mind I could work out how changes in my
line would affect the way the bike was working. If I went into a corner a
little tighter here in order to come out faster, that would make second
gear work a bit better, and so on. We didn't have gearboxes to change on
the 700s, so that sort of thing was very important then.

I went back out on the track and broke the lap record on about the third
lap. It had all been done in my head. From that day I started doing a lot more
work in my mind. It had been forced on me then because of the short practice time but since then I have used that method all the time. It is the only
way really to sort out what you are doing. The effect it had at Brands
shocked me and I even used it back in America for my dirt track racing.

When I first did Grands Prix in '78 I used to read *Motocourse*, because
that would give me an idea of what to expect from the next race track. I
would go there with a rough idea and then walk the track to fix it in my
mind. You have to be able to run through the track in your mind as though
you are watching a video screen with pictures taken from the bike –
recall it as you saw it when you were riding round.

I had to take track learning seriously because I had done less than twenty road races when I first went to Europe and, as Kel pointed out, I was going to get killed if I didn't work out exactly where I was going. Kel was good at making me realise how dangerous it could be, going out there and trying to beat everybody and getting in way over my head. He was conscious of the fact that European race tracks can be very dangerous, with no run-off, and was pointing out that I had to learn *where* I was going before I tried to go fast.

When race tracks are dangerous you have to pick and choose which corners you are going to ride flat out on and where you are going to keep something in reserve. Through a particularly dangerous corner I might only go at 95 per cent. Of course most of the others might only go at 90 per cent. It all depends on the trust you have in your own ability.

For example, there was a fast right-hander after the start and finish at the Salzburgring. It has now been changed, with a chicane, but it used to be flat out on the 500 at about 170 mph with the guard rail right on the outside. You could take it flat out if you did it exactly right, especially in the early days. When the bikes got faster it became more difficult, but even in '83 I could do it almost flat out.

I wouldn't go flat out for more than two or three laps at a time, though, but when I did it meant I could stretch a second and a half or two seconds a lap, like I did in '78. It had to be right, because it was dangerous, but I knew that I had the concentration and the ability to do those three laps in a row, and by doing that I could open up a lead. Then it'd be back down to only 90 or 95 per cent round that corner and just hold on to the lead. I could not do it for the whole race, because I would not have had the strength, timing and concentration to do it every lap, and to try would have been risky.

It was a good place to make up time. Dangerous, but if everyone else was going to go through there at 95 per cent and I could make it at 100 per cent, and still be within the bounds of what was safe for me, then it was fine. It is a lot easier to make up time on fast corners.

That corner in Austria is like a lot of others in that it is *where you come out* that is most important. You have to be able to see your exit line and know what you have to do to get to it. See it, then do it. If you have the timing and the strength it will work out for you. If you cannot visualise the corner in your mind, and see the exit when you are going in, you will be making it up as you go round and there is no way that you can compensate fast enough to make a good job of it. See it all as you go in. Have everything planned in your mind.

I think that one of the reasons why I was so good at the beginning of the season, compared with the Europeans, was that I had been training on dirt bikes all winter and my muscles and my mind were fresh and ready to race. Not only was I physically ready to race but my mind didn't need time to get up to speed. I had been practising the process of seeing the line and following it all through the winter with my usual training programme.

When it comes to learning a track and seeing the line to use, you must pick a brake marker but not a peeling-off point. It is the brake marker that dictates where you peel off. Daytona is a good example. I used to go down the back straight and shut off at the 180-yard point, or 200 yards depend-

Roberts learnt a great deal about picking a line while dirt track racing. He discovered the importance of having the bike in the right place early in the corner so as to get the best, straightest drive out. On the dirt, picking a line is more complicated because of the greater variation in traction. This is the '76 San José Mile and Roberts needs the good drive as the Yamaha is chasing the Harleys of Ted Boody, Steve Eklund and Roberts's arch rival Gary Scott. After this fierce battle Roberts finished fifth and came within a point of eliminating himself from the title chase, while eventual champion Jay Springsteen increased his advantage with a win.

Walter Villa was on his way to his first 250 World Championship on the Aermacchi Harley-Davidson when Roberts arrived at Assen for his first Grand Prix. It was the fourth Grand Prix of 1974 and Villa had already won at Imola. The American set the fastest time in practice, demonstrating that he had picked some good lines round the long, tortuous circuit. Elsewhere, Roberts explains the mistake that possibly cost him the race.

ing on which way the wind was blowing. As I arrived there I couldn't see a thing. There was so much buffeting and vibration that I couldn't bring the corner into focus, but I knew that by the time I'd slowed enough to get into third gear it was time to flick the bike into the turn.

All you concentrate on is the braking. The same is true at Paul Ricard, down the back straight. I'd brake at my marker, not too severely at first because at that speed the rise and fall of the road makes the back end light, then harder and knock it back two gears, then flick it in. I can't visually see a peel-off point because I am already looking through the corner for the exit point on the far kerb so that I can get on the gas. I can envisage where I want to be as I peel off, but if I am looking at that point I'm going too slowly.

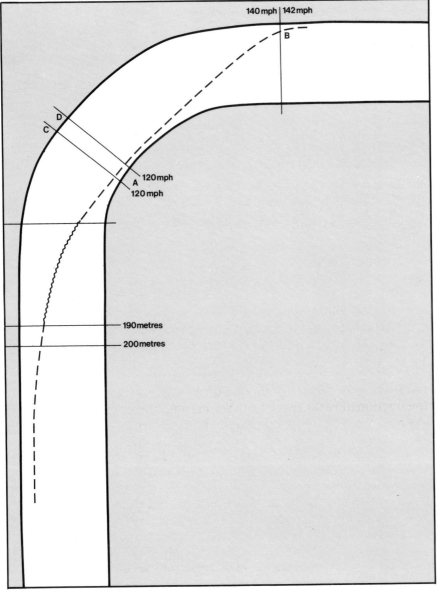

You can work out how to get through a corner faster – and, more importantly, how to get on the next straight at higher speed – by identifying the point in the corner at which you have to get back on the gas. Take that corner at Ricard at the end of the back straight. Say I need to be doing 120 mph when I start to accelerate (A) in order to reach 140 mph as I hit the kerb on the exit (B). Any more than 120 mph as I hit that point (A), and I am going to hit that kerb doing only 137, because I am going to be leant over too far. I will not be able to accelerate and keep accelerating out of the turn in the same way. Somewhere I am going to have to roll it back or I'll run off the track.

So this is how I would approach the situation. I'm shutting off at 200 and braking severely. It takes me a little time to get the bike on its side (C-D). I know that I cannot save much time in this section of the corner unless I can get better tyres or make improvements to the bike. However, you can gain extra speed by moving the point in the corner at which you do certain things. What I might be able to do is to shorten the braking distance and brake at 190. This means I will flick the bike in harder and later which will shorten that segment of the corner (C-D). This will allow me to start accelerating again at an earlier point and I might reach 142 mph as I hit the kerb on the exit.

From 120 mph to the exit I have a traction problem and the back tyre could spin. If it spins it slows me down, so that limits how fast I can accelerate. In the preceding section I have no traction problem, I flick the bike so fast and so violently all the weight goes onto the front tyre and I turn. As soon as the bike settles and about 40 per cent of the weight comes onto the back tyre I am on the gas again. Not fully at first but more and more as the weight goes on and I feel for traction.

A lot of guys are so slow to turn and so slow to get on the throttle that the front end will push. The front end will never slide with the power on, once you get above idle. I've never pushed the front tyre on a high speed corner like this because even if it starts to go I am on the throttle so soon that it will not go anywhere.

There are people who can go into the turn faster than me, but they will be doing 123 in the middle and only 137 on the way out and that is no good. It will hurt your speed all the way to the next corner.

The problem really is that the machine does not want to turn when it comes to the end of the straight. With all that straight line speed and mass, the spinning wheels acting as gyros all wanting to go straight on, the last thing that the motor cycle wants to do is have you force the right handle-bar out so that it will fall into the turn. Getting the bike to turn in quickly is hard but critically important. You don't consciously push on that inside bar. It is a natural reaction, a very forceful, violent action that will be tough on your arms and upper body. Anyone who is going to ride a 500 hard will need a very strong upper body.

How you make the transition from braking to turning depends on what sort of corner it is. On a high speed corner, like the one at Paul Ricard we have been discussing, you want to be coming off the brakes as you flick it in. The bike should still be kneeling on the front wheel as you turn in, so it is low and turns in easily. If you let the brakes off completely before you start to turn the bike will come up and want to go straight on. You need to flick the bike while the centre of gravity is lower and the steering head is steeper, just before you let the brakes off.

There are slower, longer corners where you can still be doing some braking as you turn. But the ideal is that you should be off the brakes and over to the maximum lean in the shortest possible time, so there is no rolling into the corner on the brakes.

The ultimate is to get the braking and flicking over in the shortest time. I want to have my eyes out looking for the exit point on the far kerb and my backside feeling for the traction from the rear wheel. You can flick the bike in with the rear end still in the air. You can't do that with the wheel way off the ground, but if it is dancing around a bit that is not going to hurt you – it will follow the front as you flick it in. To make more certain that the back wheel will be on the ground you can get on the back brake just at, or just before, the braking marker.

If I go into the corner too hot all the rest of the plan means nothing. Miss these points and you will be trying to recover all through the corner and be way too slow coming out. Someone else might be able to go into the corner faster than me, he might outbrake me and go past on the inside, but will he make those important reference points? I don't think he will – and then I will be passing him back down the next straight.

A downhill right-hander

'This is the downhill corner that makes the front end push so bad. Braking deep into this really makes you hold your breath because it is so hard to shorten the section of the corner where you are on the brakes and turning but you can't apply the power to unload that front tyre. This means you have to work even harder than usual at getting the bike turned and pointed in the right direction. It is not the place for being brave and rushing deep into the corner on the brakes. You might make up a little time going in but you will certainly lose it again coming out and you might fall down while you are at it. If it is going to push, you want to find out early so you have time to do something about it. Flick it early and don't get in too deep.'

You have to pick out the soft corners from the hard corners. The so. corners are those where the line does not make a lot of difference, such as the next long, looping, right-hander at Ricard.

The fast left- and right-hander after the start and finish at Ricard was the type of corner I excelled at. This one has nothing to do with practice. It depends purely on how strong you are, how good your timing is and therefore how quickly you can go from the left-hander across to the right and then back for the little left on the exit. If my tyres went off it did not make any difference because you are not leant over to the max with the power on; I could make up so much time through the corner that I could ease off a little coming out if I had a traction problem.

That right-hander of those esses is very bumpy on the inside. Some riders try and miss those bumps, but the only fast way is to go through them with the power on. I always had the bike set up with a steep steering head angle, and it would wobble and shake halfway round the race track, but if I could get through those esses three-tenths of a second quicker I didn't care if it wobbled for 200 yards. I just wound the steering damper up as hard as I could.

The steering damper helped stop the bike from wobbling, but it didn't slow the rate at which I could flick the bike into the corner. The steering damper will stop the bike from going into a terminal shake, but there is no way you can turn the bike that fast at high speed so the damper will never slow you down. It would while you rode round the paddock at walking pace, but not at high speed on the race track because it is a hydraulic damper and the oil will move through it at a certain speed.

It was forcing the bike to turn so fast that eventually did my right forearm in. In the end I needed an operation to remove scarred tissue, because years of wrenching at the bike had wrecked the muscle. It had grown to be too big for the sheath that wraps around it.

The power to wrestle the bike is all-important. You can go quite fast without it, but when it comes to that last second that makes the difference between winning and coming third or fourth then you have to be strong. Christian Sarron can ride the bike fast but you hardly ever see him racing with Freddie Spencer or Eddie Lawson. There is a point in being as big as Rob McElnea, because he can dominate the motor cycle, but there is a minus as well because he weighs so much and blocks so much wind down the straight. Freddie is not heavy and is probably not all that strong in his arms but he is nearly a foot taller than me and can use that extra leverage to make up for it. I could still get through chicanes faster and outbrake him because I think I was a little stronger.

The track at Silverstone is so wide that on most corners the line is not vital to within a few feet, but even there there are certain kerbs that you have to touch to use all the road. The uphill left-hander towards the last corner complex is one and so is the left-hander onto the back straight. I could always come through there on the gas, even though the tyres were often not 100 per cent.

The old Woodcote was a corner where you had to go in a little slower and then get the gas on. You would arrive in sixth and knock it back two, then on the power. You had to run across the bumps and, because I had my bike set up hard at Silverstone, perhaps I lost a little ground there. But

Exiting Woodcote corner at Silverstone, Roberts leads Sheene across the line to win the 1979 British Grand Prix. The approach to Woodcote has since been slowed by a chicane but at this high-speed circuit at which Roberts excelled the exit from this corner has lost none of its importance.

An S-bend

'This S-bend section is downhill and in any downhill corner the bike will have a tendency to push the front more than normal. That means that more than ever you have to get on the power early in the corner so that it does not run away from you.

'You are not going to make up that much time with speed out of the first turn because it is followed by another corner. You don't want to be too slow on the brakes or through the corner but it is more important not to foul yourself up for the second part of the corner which leads out onto the straight.

'It is vital to get a decent drive out of the first corner so that you can use the throttle to help you change direction and get set up into the second corner. If you are late getting on the gas out of the first part, you will be late on the brakes and late turning for the second. By messing up one corner, you will have messed up two – and the entry onto the straight.'

Woodcote wasn't a corner that I thought could make you a lot of time. You couldn't see round it but you had to know where the exit was. As soon as you picked out the grass on the exit you had to be wide open. You could have been hard on the gas ten feet further back, if you had been able see the exit, but you couldn't so there was no sense in worrying about it. Of course, the more you rode there the better you got at it, but it was one of those corners that is pretty hard to do first time out.

A problem a lot of guys have is knowing where to go fast. That double right-hander before the left that leads onto the back straight at Ricard is one of those corners that only leads to the next corner, and there are many on different race tracks. Go faster through there and all you are going to do is mess up the entrance into the next turn. It can be tough to figure out where to go slow and where to go fast. That's something that Kel taught me. Don't go through a corner at 100 per cent if the next corner is more important. It just means that you will be leant over longer, and if you cannot be in the right place on the race track to get it from right to left, then you will have to shut the throttle and lose momentum.

I learnt that back in 1974, when I first raced the 250 at Assen. Kel pointed out corners where I should not go too fast because it was just going to slow me down through the next corner. After I had slid off at the hairpin, through slipping the clutch, I got back on and caught up to the second-place man, Bruno Kneubühler, who was on another Yamaha. He was real fast through the left-hand fifth corner but that just made him slower through the next right and, as Kel had told me, the second one was more important. I thought, if this guy is second in Europe then he has a lot to learn. I guess he has since then.

That lesson showed me a lot about going slow to go fast. It is very difficult to judge just how slow to go. What I used to do was to run the bike up to a certain rpm, or rush up to a marker and close the throttle, to discipline myself into only going at a certain speed. That's real hard to do, though, because as you get into the race, and get lapping quicker and quicker, the temptation is to push the bike harder into the corner and get in there faster, but in fact you end up going slower where it counts. The really key thing to going faster is to keep that slower corner under control. If I need to go through that corner at 40 I must go through it at 40 every time. I don't want to go through it at 42, because that means that through the next corner and out onto the straight I am going to be slower. If you work out that you have to be slower than 100 per cent through a corner, stick to it.

Chapter 4

Braking

When I am braking very very hard I am in a trance, concentrating on nothing but the braking. I don't even watch the track. I seem to be looking at the tach., travelling too fast to focus on the road, but I know how long it takes to slow and when I have changed into the right gear I look up and bring the track into focus. There are not many places where the braking is that severe. Daytona is one. Normally you are more aware of what is going on around you. But you should still be concentrating 100 per cent on braking.

I worked hard at setting up the bike to brake hard. Early on during my Grand Prix career we had problems with the forks. We had springs made in two halves, of different winds. If we were working with forks that gave six inches of travel we would have a choice of three different springs for the first three inches, and another three possible springs for the next half of the stroke. It gave us a good amount of variation in the spring rates we could have and that, along with altering the damping oil level, allowed a fair degree of adjustment in the forks.

I always liked to have a little bit of travel left, even under heavy braking, to allow for hitting a bump. By playing around with the two spring rates we could normally get what I wanted.

One good reason for keeping the forks from bottoming is that your back wheel will come off the ground when the front forks bottom. Most factories have tried some sort of anti-dive to stop the forks bottoming out. Anti-dive would be OK if it still allowed the suspension to work. But the systems I have used locked up the suspension, so we always had them adjusted back to the point where they were not working at all. The trouble is that this affected the damping oil flow and not the springing.

Instead we had the two springs, and inside the first spring we would have a spacer tube, so that after two inches of travel the weight came down on the spacer and that put the load on the second spring. I could adjust it as necessary, with a different length spacer if I needed it, or a different spring. In the case of a track with a lot of ripples I could have a soft spring on the first two inches. That is where you should be operating when the throttle is above idle, where the weight is coming onto the back wheel. The soft spring lets the wheel move easily over the bumps; then, once into the. corner and onto the gas, it stops the front end skittering around all over.

On a real high speed track where there was no heavy braking we might find we were only using four out of the six inches of travel. So then we would soften the springing. Even if there is only one corner with heavy braking you have to ask yourself the question, 'Are you going to mess up those faster, more important corners just because you are getting out of shape braking for one slow corner?' You want to use the travel if you need it, but you don't want the forks bottoming out where the braking and the bumps are so bad that you can't keep control going into the corners on the brakes.

At a track like Silverstone, which has fast corners and needs a lot of cornering force, we would use a stiffer first spring so that it only compressed between two and three inches and still left travel to cope with the bumps.

I used to set the bike up stiffer at bumpy circuits because I always felt it was better to have the bike take the bump and not have it sagging, going through the corner. The more the suspension has to move, the more the damping goes away – at least that was the problem I used to have with the monoshock system that I had to put up with for most of my career, until I started to work with Ohlins and my life changed completely. With better suspension systems the problem of fading damping is not so bad. But once the damping goes away you have a ride that is totally unpredictable. You have to slow down, and I had to do that just too often in my career before we got decent suspension.

I like the brakes to have a little bit of give in them, because the closer I can get the lever to the handlebar, the more pressure I can put on them. If the lever is way out then you cannot get a good grip on it. I brake with two fingers, which leaves me with the two smaller fingers on the throttle. To allow some slack in the lever you need good brakes. It is no good starting with a little bit of movement if the lever will be back to the bar after a couple of laps.

To match the amount of brake movement with the leverage you need, you have to put the right handlebar piston size with the right brake caliper piston sizes. We kept going to larger front disc sizes because they helped to stop the bike, and it also helped when we went to smaller front wheels, because of the ratio of tyre size to disc size.

With two fingers left on the throttle I can go from braking to accelerating in no time. The gas should be on for as long as possible so I can start rolling on the throttle as I begin to ease off the brake, taking the weight off the front wheel and putting it on the back.

I do use the rear brake, but only a little. Sometimes I use it just to bring down the back a bit, before I hit the front brake, but not too much. If I was getting into a corner a little too hot and I felt there was a risk of the front end pushing, I would use the rear brake a little. But I'd only do that if I had got into trouble and I was worried about the front, and there was no room to pick the bike up and get the throttle on.

I use the back brake in the rain. There isn't the same weight transfer onto the front as there is in the dry, so the rear brake can do a little more work. In the dry there is almost no weight on the back wheel when the front brake is hard on, stopping from high speed and you can use what little weight there is on the back with the engine braking, to feel the engine as you change down through the gears.

Braking

'This is not the perfect braking shot because it was a cold, miserable day and I was not flicking it in like I normally would. I should have been turning quicker as I got off the brakes and not just rolling it in, but this is still a good corner for seeing how the bike behaves on maximum brakes. The front tyre is fully compressed and the rear tyre is almost off the ground, right up to the point where you flick it on its side.

'These pictures show how important it is to have the turning of the bike off pat. You don't have time to think about what you are doing, you have to be thinking ahead of the bike, thinking through the corner to the point where you are going to get on the gas.'

Even on a two stroke the engine is also used to slow the bike: you don't realise how much until you don't have the use of the engine. I found that out the last time I rode a 500. It was at Laguna Seca and part of the gearchange mechanism kept working its way out and fouling the gearchange. There I was, coming up the back straight at Laguna in fifth gear and arriving at the Corkscrew, which is a second-gear corner, to find that it wouldn't change. When it first happened I thought about pulling in. Then Randy started to get away and it began working again, so I carried on. I started catching Randy, but out it came again and jammed. This kept happening and it was pretty wild because I was having to brake so hard that the front wheel was hopping off the ground. It started over the ripples and carried on because all the suspension was already used up. It got so bad that the front wheel seemed like it was off the ground half the time on the brakes. I just held the lever on until I had slowed enough. I thought I could make the corner the next time and when the front tyre hit the road I'd flick it in. I got quite good at it, and managed it about six times, but finally I said, 'That's it, it is not going to get better', and I eased up. I had been trying to keep up, hoping that if it was a nut or something that would fall all the way out then I would be close enough to Randy to pass him before the end. When I realised that it wasn't going to clear up I cruised.

When I change gears, I let the clutch out between changes. I have tried just pulling the clutch in and doing all the changes at once, but I never reckoned on it. If you don't know exactly what you are doing, what gear you are in and what engine speed you should have, you are never going to be able to go to Daytona and brake as late as the 180-yard marker for the chicane. The one occasion that you arrive at the corner in the wrong gear or in neutral is not worth it. When you come to let the clutch out after changing down three gears in one go you might just have changed too many gears, or have too little engine speed as you go to tip it into the corner, and the back end will start to come around. Let the clutch out between each gearchange, just for a fraction, and you can feel what gear you are in and what the engine is doing. You will know exactly where you are as you come to let the clutch out in the right gear for the corner, and get on the gas.

I remember making a mistake about which gear I was in at my very first Grand Prix. I went to Assen with the same brakes on my 250 as were on my 700, and I could lock up that little bike anywhere. It was my first push-start and I got away slowly, but I caught Villa on the Harley, he was leading. I just wanted to pass him to show him I could do it, because I knew it would screw him up. At the end of the main straight there was this first-gear right and I whipped out of his draft and went past on the brakes. The trouble was, I didn't get it all the way down to first and, as I went round the corner, I realised it was in second so I grabbed the clutch, slipped it and spun the bike out right in front of him – almost knocked him off. I learned my lesson there. Kel had told me: 'Whatever you do, don't slip the clutch.' I never did it again. It had happened because I was so determined to outbrake him. I had set myself up for it.

If you can keep away from the bumps on the brakes it may well be worth it. It depends how much it affects your line for the corner and the way you have the suspension set up. If you have decided that you need

Graeme McGregor demonstrates the result of too much front brake, too deep into the corner at Assen on his 350 Yamaha. McGregor was always hard on the brakes, which made him a very competitive racer and he recovered from this fall to go on to greater success, including

second place in the Belgian Grand Prix at Spa in '82 behind Toni Mang. Roberts points out that those who push the front hard are likely to suffer the front end tucking under, just as McGregor did, and from this position it's hard to stay on two wheels.

the softer suspension, which bottoms out on the brakes, then try taking the smoother line and find out if it is any slower. It is worth trying three laps each way in practice, to see which works best. The other consideration is the length of the race. Can you last longer by going through the bumps or around them? Braking over the bumps can be hard on the forearms and in a long race it might be a good bet to miss them if you can.

If the tank suits you properly, and you can squeeze it with your knees, you can hold some of the pressure off your forearms and that means you

90-degree corner

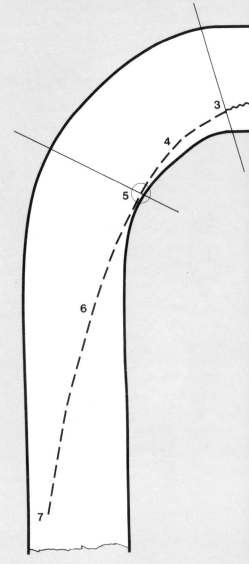

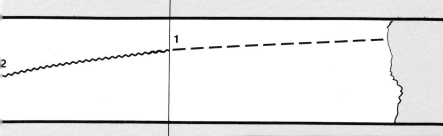

1

2

Kenny Roberts describes the technique used by a top rider (in this case Mike Baldwin) to take a 90-degree corner: 'At this point (1), you're hard on the brakes, maximum pressure, so that the weight is all on the front wheel and the front suspension is compressed. All the rider's weight is on his arms. (2) Still braking hard in a straight line, but getting ready to pitch the bike on its side. (3) The transition point from maximum braking to maximum turn-rate. This must be completed in as short a distance as possible. This is where you can make up time, while you're getting the bike turned in the right direction. (4) Pulling the bike down and getting back on the power to help it turn. Get the throttle off idle so that the front end doesn't push. (5) Here, at the apex, you should already be pointing in the right direction. The power is coming in as you are straightening the bike for a direct drive down the straight. (6) The power should be coming in hard because you are no longer worrying about the corner, all that work has been done. You should just be feeling for grip with the back end under maximum acceleration. (7) Let the bike run out to the white line and use all the road – without fighting to keep it on the track. If you are having to hold off the throttle because you are running out of road then you've blown it.'

can control the bike better. You need all your strength to flick the bike on its side. There is no sense in wasting energy pushing on the bars while you are braking, if you can spread the load. You need a tank that fits you well, so that it takes the load from your knees but still lets you move across the seat as you go into the turn.

Everyone uses their body as an air brake, sitting up as they hit the brakes so that the chest takes the wind and slows the bike. Don't forget that, in the same way, you have to get down out of the wind as soon as you have stopped braking and want to get going through the corner. That will make a lot of difference, especially on high-speed tracks like Silverstone and Paul Ricard. It is wasting engine power if you wait until you are through the corner before you get down behind the bubble.

When it comes to trying to pass people on the brakes, a lot depends on what the other guy is doing. If you are braking pretty late anyway, and the other guy is still going to get to the corner first, you have to weigh up whether to let your brakes off for a second and go past, or let him make a fool of himself by going into the corner too fast so that you can go underneath him on the way out. It's never been a big thing for me, to force past someone underneath, going into the corner on the brakes. I would rather brake a bit earlier, turn, and get past going out of the corner. It is safer and you have that extra speed all the way down the next straight, so he won't get past you again. There are times when it is the best or only way to get past, though, and if it comes down to a last-lap effort going past on the brakes can be a very tricky decision. Can you risk falling down just to win the race? If you fall down, you get nothing.

A good case in point is the way I set Spencer up at the Swedish GP in '83. I thought we had that race lost before we got there, because the Honda was so manoeuvrable and I couldn't see where the V four had any advantage I could use to beat him. The straights are so short and the corners so tight at Anderstorp that I thought he would be round them on the gas while I was still fighting with the four.

It turned out to be a close race, though, and I realised we were going to be right together on the last lap. I had been using an early brake marker at the end of the straight and, on the last lap, I sat up at that point but I didn't brake. Then I sank back behind the bubble. I knew that as he was drafting me he would see me sit up and think I was braking and that it was time to flick out to the side and go past. He did, but I carried on as far as I dared go and then braked. Everything was OK until he found out that he wasn't out-braking me. He then let go of the brakes and, just as I peeled off into the corner, he came past up the inside – upright and still with his brakes on. I had to pick the bike up and make a second go at it; I had no choice because I was turning into him. He wasn't even close to making the corner because he was only thinking about getting past me. There was no room to make it round, at the angle we were heading into the corner, but I wasn't thinking about winning the race at that point, just avoiding a crash.

Off the race track we both went. I had no idea what the dirt was like but I stayed upright. If he had crashed he would have looked a big idiot but, as it was, he was on the inside and got back on the race track before I did and won the race. The week after everyone had forgotten that he took us both off the circuit.

The braking contest with Freddie Spencer at the end of the Anderstorp main straight was bad news for Roberts's chances of winning the '83 World Championship. 'I underestimated just how far he would go to win,' he said later. Roberts went off the tarmac and Spencer got the drive to the last corner and the flag. It was a race in which Roberts should never have stood a chance, as the Honda was expected to be far superior round and out of the tight corners, but he battled wheel-to-wheel with Spencer all the way.

You don't have to leave the late braking or the overtaking to the very last corner, of course. Maybe it is better to pick a different corner, because you know that in the four corners after that there is no way he can get past you again. I had Spencer lined up that way earlier the same year, at the Spanish Grand Prix at Jarama. I knew exactly where I wanted to pass him. It was on the brakes and I had everything dialled in – except that Middelburg and another three guys were there when I wanted to make the move. The difficulty that year was that the four was not manoeuvrable and if there was anyone on my line I was in trouble. With those other guys there I had had it.

You should never show the other guy what you can do until you are ready to make the move or he will block it by using the inside piece of road. That was true of the run-in with Freddie in Sweden. If I had thought for one minute he would do something that stupid I would have gone to the inside and blocked his move. The only way to pass someone in that situation is to slingshot him and brake late enough to get right alongside him. If you are level with him and on the inside you have to make the corner first. Arriving up the inside just as he peels off is no way to pass anybody. That is desperation. I let him know how I felt about it afterwards, when they drove us round the circuit in the victory car.

There are certain times when you might be forced to use the front brake at a corner, if you have got in too hot. You don't want to put the front brake on in the middle of the corner, because it will make the bike sit up and run wide. Some bikes do it more than others. You should try to hold it down tight and get the bike turned – the last thing you want to be is running off wide, which is what can happen if you get on the brakes while you are leant over. It is not to be recommended, as it is not the fastest way round the race track, but if you feel you are going too fast you can reach up and finesse the front brake and the back brake. I have done it, but obviously it is something you try and avoid because if you are going into the corner hard there isn't a lot of traction left for braking.

There are corners, double radius ones, which force you to brake while you are leaned over. If that happens I still like to get on the brakes a little sooner – not too hard on the front – but get the throttle open earlier. If the corner is such that you have to brake, then that is what you must concentrate on, and you have to be prepared for the front to push.

Riders who do all their braking going into the corner are asking for trouble. Pushing and pushing the front will make you come unstuck sooner or later. There are guys who can ride on the brakes going into the turn. Sheene was good at it, and Mackenzie does it and goes fast, but he also falls down because it is hard to save the front when it starts to tuck under. It is much easier to do your braking early and get on the power. You can feel for traction with the back end and the consequences of sliding are nowhere near as bad.

I would say that braking is not a place to make up a lot of time. Most of the desperate brakers I have come across screwed themselves up more than anything. Hansford was as good on the brakes as anyone I have ever seen, and it does seem that Australians and New Zealanders are good at braking because they have tight race tracks. Crosby was good on the brakes, like Hansford, and they were both fast. But it's not the way I liked to ride.

The OW61 was the first of the V fours and a fearsome weapon. Belgian Grand Prix at Spa, 1982: the World Championship had reached a crucial stage with Franco Uncini leading Roberts by three points. A win would, at the least, have made things even and when Roberts took the lead on lap three he set out to destroy the opposition. However, the combination of engine characteristics, frame and suspension created a violent beast of a motor cycle and the tyres were soon destroyed. From lap eight things went downhill for Roberts and here Spencer lines him up approaching the hairpin before the start of lap nine, during the course of which he would take the lead, going on to win his first Grand Prix. La Source hairpin is a classic test of braking performance.

Most top-class riders are just about equal at a dead-stop hairpin, as long as the bikes all have about the same braking performance. At a hairpin the line is not so critical. If you were good enough to take three bike lengths out of me on the brakes and hold it while we were accelerating out of the hairpin, I would say you had an advantage. But I have not had that many people do it to me. I'd maintain that late braking is no big thing when it comes to being fastest round a race track – but you might just need it on the last lap if you haven't managed to get in front.

Chapter 5

Style

I raced a dirt tracker from the age of fourteen, but it was not until I was eighteen that I got on a road racer. By then I was already number one novice dirt tracker in the States. I was lucky because I had a good basic knowledge of controlling a motor cycle at speed, without ever wanting to race on pavement.

There is no way that dirt track racing is the same as road racing. The great thing about dirt track, though, is that when you are starting you can learn about controlling the motor cycle at much slower speeds, at much less risk. You can learn just to ride a road racer right from the start, and you can do it very well. It's done in Europe and Sheene proved that he could be World Champion even though he didn't have the opportunity to ride dirt track. But the advantage of a dirt tracker is that you can ride the bike out of control and not fall off. You can't do that, you don't have that luxury on a road racer.

I was young and when Jim Doyle said I should ride a road racer I went to Daytona and rode his bike without even thinking about it. I had never even seen a road racer before. I only did a couple of laps and never thought much about it, but later, when it was settled that I was going to ride for Yamaha, they wanted me to have a go at road racing because that is what dirt trackers did to get more points for the National Championship. There were only a couple of guys, like Nixon and Rayborn, who were good at road racing. Nixon had been number one but Calvin specialised in road racing even though he won a lot of dirt races, mostly miles.

I just jumped on a road racer at Vaccoville. I don't think they even race there any more. I won that race with the Yamaha 350 going away. It was an AFM club race and I thought, 'Well, this is easier than dirt track.' I didn't put my foot down and things just went like clockwork. I went faster and faster until the bike started detonating and I slowed down.

I went to another race at Orange County and I couldn't make the corners, I was going into them so fast. At the end of the straight there was a corner with a post and a walkway onto the exit. I was going around the post and using the walkway because I couldn't stay on the track coming out, and at the next right-hander I threw it away. I'd gone in there and lost it and I didn't even know why. I thought, 'Damn, what did I do?' I got a slight concussion out of that and I was standing on the race track and couldn't see anything. I knew not to move in case someone ran into me.

I guess I had learnt the hard way that road racing wasn't quite as easy as I had thought first time out. After that I slowed down. I went to Daytona

The Roberts road racing style evolved out of the rear-end slide that turns a dirt tracker so quickly. Here he lets it all hang out at the Houston Astrodome on the indoor short track – the scene of many triumphs but not this time as the single-cylinder two stroke seized because of an air leak when he was well on his way to victory.

and then I thought about it and said to myself, 'Well, I am going to learn how to do this right.' Of course all the advice was to slow down: 'Kenny, you can't do this overnight.' I realised I had to slow down and think about it a bit more or I was going to kill myself. I got tenth in the 350 class, I think, and in the 250 I broke down.

I went to the next road race – I was junior expert I guess – and I rode the 350 and won, but I still didn't know anything about road racing. I really wasn't learning anything except that if I went too fast I fell off. I wasn't adapting to the road racer, I was just riding it without really progressing. We did very few road races and I was still riding sitting straight up and down on the bike, but I did OK and I guess I was the best young kid coming up.

What made the difference was that Kel had arrived from Europe and he signed on at Yamaha to ride and head the team. He helped me. I started learning about lines, and slow and fast corners – to go fast through fast corners because that is where you make up the most time, and go slow through the slow corners.

I had a friend, Bill Robinson, who sold Goodyear tyres back east in Florida and he knew Cal Rayborn and worked with him. Bill and I got to be good friends and he would tell me stories about how Calvin used to set his bike up. Bill was a real enthusiast. He knew everybody and everyone respected him. He started helping me and we would run around together, drive his truck to races, and he would help me with my tyre selection, telling me what to run and what was not going to work.

I learnt in that way but I didn't start using my dirt track experience until slicks came out. About the time Goodyear started making slicks I started sliding the back end a bit. Up to then I thought that road racing and dirt track were different and didn't see any connection. I was riding with Kel and he was fast, so I copied him up to that point. Then I said to him, 'Hey, you can slide the back end a bit.' Kel said, 'No, you don't want to slide that back end, if the back slides there is something wrong. If you slide the back end too far you are going to crash.' I never forgot something that Bill Robinson told me, that Cal Rayborn used to set his bike up to oversteer in the fast corners and understeer in the slow corners. I used to think about that a lot, because Cal was one of my heroes and he used to like to slide the bike round the faster corners and let it push a bit on the slower corners. That was the way I ended up with my bike, pushing in the slow corners, just a little bit, but in the faster stuff I would be on the gas and starting to slide it. When I started to slide the back end I found it was real uncomfortable to do it sitting straight up and down. I could never get it to work right. There was just something I felt was wrong.

I saw pictures of Jarno Saarinen in Europe and Kel told me he was a really good guy, a hot shoe. He came to America in '71 and I thought, 'Well, I have got to find out why this guy is so good', because I wanted to be good. He wanted to set the bike up different from us, it seemed really odd. He wanted a stock swing arm on the bike whereas we had two-inch longer swing arms that Kel had made for us. He wanted a stock motor and had weird handlebars that he brought with him. I couldn't understand how he could be so fast when his ideas were so out of wack. How could this guy be so fast when he had a stock swing arm and so on when

The two arch-rivals comparing styles. Crunch time in 1983: Roberts could still have stolen the title from Spencer with a win in the final race of the season at Imola, provided the Honda finished third or lower. Both shift their weight well to the inside but Spencer's hips pivot more.

The approach to a left-hand corner

'Here is a point where you don't want to use all the road coming out of the right-hander so that you can get on the gas and lined up for the heavy braking down to the next left. You might use all the road out of the right if you wanted a faster drive down to the next left to go underneath someone into the last corner – but all you are going to do then is steal his line and spoil your own coming out of the second left.

'I always used a bit more road than this coming out of the right-hander and Mike would be using more road in a race, but this is a test day and he is not going quite so fast. However, you can see the importance of a straight line between the two corners so that you can get the hard braking done straight up and down. You don't want long wide lines out of one corner and into the next. Instead, square them off, make straight lines between the corners to get maximum acceleration and braking.'

Roberts developing the hang-off style while 250 rivals Ron Pierce on his Kawasaki and Pat Hennen on his Yamaha still sit straight up and down. Kenny found that sliding off the bike and dragging his knee on the ground gave him better control, even if some thought it pretty wild at first.

Fully developed, the Roberts style became a classic to which others were compared. Here he demonstrates the variation used on the 250 at Riverside in 1976. He won the AMA National Championship race that day on the 750 Yamaha and kept his title hopes alive a little longer.

everyone in America had Kel's swing arm? When we got to Ontario I found out why he was so fast, because I was sliding all over the place. I could not get enough traction. My 250 was working good, it just had a little longer swing arm, but the 350 had the engine further forward and had the two-inch longer swing arm. The year before, when Kel built the bike, it needed it. Then Yamaha changed things but Kel still ran the old frame.

I put my 350 engine in my 250 frame, which was basically standard, and I found I had a lot more traction. Kel ended up doing the same thing because at Ontario we just couldn't get the bike to hook up. The fact that it worked made me think a lot about things. Before I'd never thought much, I never changed anything, except maybe mess around with the shocks. I just used to get on and ride. But Ontario made me think about my style, and how come Jarno hung off like that, or at least laid down on the gas tank and slid his body off to the side a bit.

There was one corner that was a big second-gear loop. In the middle of it, while sitting straight up and down on the bike, I felt that the front end was going to slide away. I couldn't carry enough speed through the corner to be safe: by the middle of the turn I had slowed down too much and it was too early to gas it because the tyres were not good enough. It scared me. I was racing with Kel and I decided to hang off, so I slid my butt off to the side and went round. It didn't feel so great for the first few laps but pretty soon it began to feel good and, believe it or not, that mid-corner crisis I was having went away.

Rayborn had touched his knee twice on the tarmac in that first 125-mile leg. He lost the front end in one of the corners and fell halfway through the race. We were laughing about it after the first race and he was showing me where he had scraped the knee of his leathers. No one could believe it.

I was also thinking about the way I had started riding in the first race and decided that it certainly made a difference. In the second leg I really started going, but only hanging off in that one corner. I was leading Kel and pulling away from the guys we had been racing with in the first leg when the engine blew up. Kel asked me afterwards what the hell I had been doing, trying to imitate Paul Smart. But I just felt better riding that way and I spent all winter thinking about it. By the time I got to Daytona the next March I couldn't ride sitting straight up and down, I just had to hang off. I felt I would fall down if I didn't hang off. By the next race, which was Dallas, Texas, I was dragging my knees on the tarmac. I had to put tape over my leathers because I was wearing holes in them. Kel saw me with the tape and said, 'Well, you must be the most stupid son of a bi... I've ever seen, what are you doing?' Kel used to ride all tucked in and was sure I was going to crash. But it was comfortable.

When I started to move around like that I found I needed to alter the handlebars. I wanted them bent further down and it was pretty scientific how we went about sorting that out. I told Kel what I needed and Kel got a rubber mallet. Wham! He hit the bar until it was right. The first time the Japanese saw him do that they died.

Normal bars are eleven degrees down but by the time I went GP racing in Europe I was down to sixteen. When the OW61 came out I had to go to twenty-one degrees, and I stuck with that. It was because of the way the gas tank was set and the position of the footrests. I preferred shorter gas tanks so that I could put my weight further forward.

It's important to have the bike fitted to suit you, so that you feel comfortable. The seat must be right, with the correct amount of rubber and so on. The important thing is that the bike feels OK for you, it doesn't matter about the facts of the thing as long as it feels right. If a rider wants pink handlebar grips that's what he should have.

There are good scientific reasons why hanging off helps cornering. It does allow you to keep the tyre more upright, so that you can make use of a bigger contact patch. The more upright the bike is when you get the power on, the more control you have. If the bike is on its side the tyre will be on the edge, and when it slides you will be right off the edge of the tyre and you won't get it back. There is no set limit to how far you should lean off, though I think that sometimes Randy goes too far. Who knows where the limit might be? Five years from now everyone might be leaning off like Randy. The problem is that leaning off so much makes it slower to go from left to right, and that can be a big minus.

There are places where I had no time to climb from one side to another, like some of the tight chicanes at Imola. Then you have to work out which way is the most important. I would keep the bike more upright going in so that I could hang off on the other side for the exit. That would give me a bigger advantage because I could get a better drive coming out.

Once I started sliding the back tyre it was natural to relate this to the way I rode a dirt tracker, and that is where squaring the corner came in. It is natural for a road racer who dirt tracks to square off the corner – not that all dirt trackers square it off. I am a dirt tracker who squares off a dirt track corner a lot. When I started running the front end in a little slower, and getting the gas on earlier so that I could get that slide going, I started squaring off the corner.

You can't just square the corner off because you feel like it. You have to get the bike sliding a little to do it. You turn in hard by using the front and push the bike down on its side, but then you pick the bike up as you get on the gas and complete the turn by sliding the back end round, steering with the back wheel, not the front, once you have the power on. That is why Freddie likes the bike to come on the power suddenly, it gets the back end sliding. When he goes into the corner he turns the throttle just a little and gets the back end sliding, so that the bike is coming round to be pointing at the right angle heading for the exit. He is turning and can get on the gas harder, pointing in the right direction coming out.

When you run into the corner and flick the bike on its side, for a very brief moment all the weight is on the front tyre. You push it very hard with all the load on it but it won't slide away because, before it has a chance to, you are getting on the gas and, once the back takes off, it has all the load and the front has none. If you ride a normal style and are just going round the corner you stand much more of a chance of losing the front end, because you have it loaded for a much longer distance. If you get on the gas then you are so far over you may push the front end and fall down: you are at the wrong angle at the wrong time when you apply the throttle.

I never lost the front end. I always pushed it, but I gave it such a short time to slide that it never gave up on me. I remember in Argentina, at the

The Corkscrew

'There aren't too many corners in the world like the Corkscrew at Laguna Seca. In fact it's unique, but one thing you can say about it that holds good for a lot of other corners at other tracks is that the most important thing about the first part is to get through it in good shape to line up for the second part. You aren't going to gain anything by being fast through the first part, the left-hander, because you're going to be all messed up going down the hill through the right-hander.

'You have to get the bike stopped and turned early at the top of the hill with plenty of road left, so that you can get a good drive down the hill and through the right-hander – otherwise, you will run out of road there when you should be hard on the gas and already lining up for the next left.'

The Yugoslav Grand Prix in '81. The OW54 square four was an intermediate step between the straight four and the V and Roberts fought it all through the season. Rijeka was no exception and he chased Mamola and Lucchinelli all the way to the flag. The smooth style shown was shaken on lap 19 of the 32 when a particularly violent slide shook both feet off the rests and necessitated a dab on the ground with the right to keep the bike on its wheels.

GP in '82, we were using Dunlops and I told engineer Peter Ingley that if I made the race without losing the front end it would be a miracle. It had slid on me so many times in practice, because I was running it off the edge. The tyre had been built around Randy and the Suzuki, and he didn't lean over then as much as me.

I was flicking it over, and there was a kink where I fell off three or four times in practice, but I just never hit the ground. My leg was saving me and, as it went down, I would muscle it back up off my knee. I got quite good at that. Freddie is good at it too and at Silverstone in '83, when he rode the three-cylinder, he must have pushed fifty-five or sixty feet on his knee. I thought he was down, but he knows how to do it. The knee is down on the tarmac, and the bike is lying on it, and there is nothing you can do. I did it at Donington the last time I rode; Baldwin was behind me and it frightened the life out of him. It was down on my knee and I thought, 'Now easy, wait for it, a little slower', then I just pulled on the bars a bit and the front started to hook up again and it came back. I downshifted a couple of times and was back in the race.

On a dirt tracker you can practise all the things you need to do on a road racer, sliding front and back. If you want to push the front end, go to a certain corner where you can push the front all day, and you will learn to counter that. All you need to do is put a new tyre on the back and a bad tyre on the front and you can push the front end all day. You will learn how to back the thing in. Load up the back early, get on the throttle and get away from pushing the front. It is just a case of learning how to do it and then doing it over and over until it becomes second nature. It must become second nature. It's no good learning how to do it one afternoon, because by the time you get to the next road race and get into trouble you won't react quick enough to think about doing it right. It must become the natural thing for you to do.

Riding on a mini bike, a dirt tracker or racing anything anywhere is just like a big video game – the more you do it, the better you will get. Practice is the answer.

You learn to use your body weight on a dirt tracker, moving back to get more traction on the rear wheel, and you can do the same on a road racer. That's why Eddie has such a short gas tank, it gives him more room to move around up and down the seat. You can get up over the front, going into the corner, and put the pressure on the front fork, then scoot back coming out to get more traction on the rear. I do it all the time, that is what makes racing so physical especially for American riders who move around like that a lot. You have to have the strength to do it, and the stamina to do it, all through the race.

Sheene used to say to me, 'Why the hell do you move around on that bike so much?' I'd just say, 'Hey, I don't know, I'm just trying to find out how to do it right.'

Chapter 6

Racecraft

If you only had to race against the stopwatch then you'd be World Champion by being the fastest man out on the track by yourself. Racing isn't just about going fast on your own, though, because there are other guys out there that you have to beat, and it is not always the fastest guy in practice who wins the race. A lot of things come into beating the other guy to the line: stamina, tactics, pit signals, slipstreaming, anything that gets you in front when it counts.

Slipstreaming can be dangerous. I remember seeing Gary Fisher at Pocono misjudge it, run into the back of the bike he was chasing and end up sliding down the road on his backside. I also saw David Smith at Talladega, flat out down the back straight when the guy in front seized and Smith ran smack into the back of him. Somehow neither fell off. They were lucky, but bikes seize a lot less now than they did then.

You can slipstream slightly out to one side because the air is pushed out in quite a large bow wave, like a boat, so the area is not just right behind the tail of the lead machine. Nowadays, on 500s, slipstreaming is not such a big thing on some tracks because the bikes are so fast they make the straights seem short. But wherever you are riding and however short the circuit you can use someone's slipstream to overtake. That may be the only way you can get by someone, the only advantage you can exploit.

Of course there are circuits, like Paul Ricard and Daytona, that have long straights, where slipstreaming is important on every lap. On many tracks there is more reason to use the slipstream on a 250 than a 500 because they are slower and less powerful, and so you spend more time on the straight.

You have to watch out, especially on the first lap with a full tank of fuel, because you can get in behind a bunch of bikes off the start line and arrive at the end of the straight, going five or ten miles an hour faster than you ever did in practice, and not be able to stop.

It can happen that someone tucking into your slipstream will slow you down. It doesn't always happen, but I have felt it, and it seems to occur when your bike is geared a little off and is not really pulling because of the wind, or whatever. When you are geared to run at perhaps 11,500 or 12,500 rpm, and perhaps because of a head wind the bike will only pull 11,000 or 10,500, then the engine is not making its best power at those revs and the guy slipstreaming you can drag you back a little. You can certainly feel the other bike behind you. It makes your bike shake a bit and

you can sometimes feel it on your back so I guess it does have an effect, but not a big one.

When the bike behind whips out to pass you then you really know you are being slowed down. You feel it more on a 250, because the 500 has the power to keep going. I have geared the bike to take advantage of the slipstream, especially the 250, anticipating what might happen if the gearing was a little short and we came to a slipstreaming situation. By gearing a little tall you can make the best use of the slipstream, because with a tow your engine will rev on all the way to the red line.

We also geared to use the draft in qualifying sometimes, reasoning that if I could pick up someone's slipstream then that would help me put in a quick lap. When it came to the race we had to work out and try to antici-pate how things might go, because if we geared for a draft and then I found myself out on my own I might never get the bike up to its maximum rpm in top gear. We did quite a bit of that.

There were occasions when I had such a rocket ship that I didn't have to use the slipstream. But that doesn't happen often, especially in Grand Prix racing, and you never go out onto the track thinking that you won't use anyone's draft. It is always an advantage you can exploit. You might say, 'My bike is so fast I don't have to draft', but use the slipstream and you have even more of an advantage.

I also used slipstreaming to hang on to faster bikes. If I was gaining on the bike in front I would hang out to the side a little. I wouldn't be able to get past but I might be able to pass at the end of the straight, or at least I would have a good view of the corner coming up and my braking marker.

If you are the one being drafted then the most likely place you are going to be passed is at the end of the straight. You should be prepared for it. He will probably come by up the inside and it can be scary because suddenly there he is, taking your line. You have to keep your concentra-tion up and *know* where you are going, because he has just ducked underneath and you can't *see* your line any more. The horizon has changed and instead of looking at an empty track you are looking at the back of somebody. At that instant you have to know where *he* is at on the race track, and where *you* are. It is something to watch out for because, with someone coming underneath so fast at the end of a straight, any-where like the Salzburgring or Hockenheim, you can very easily end up running off the race track coming out of the corner. You have to know where you are at all times.

If some guy slipstreams you in the middle of the straight then all you have to do is tuck in behind. Unless his bike is a lot faster than yours he is not going to be able to get away. You do have to be aware, though, that when he comes past there may be someone else in his slipstream already. That guy should be aware of what you are likely to do, as he can see you being passed. The rider being passed will not be able to duck in too fast because, when two bikes pass, breaking the slipstream, they are pushed apart by the force of the wake and then, when that passes, the second bike can tuck in again. It is a tricky manoeuvre and all the riders have to be aware of what is going on and anticipate it.

It is not worth weaving all over the track to try and stop some guy from slipstreaming you. For one thing it is dangerous, and for another it slows you down. Every little bit of force you put on the tyres uses energy and that is energy you should be using to go forward. When I started riding at Daytona it was something I asked Kel about, and I remember him saying that every time you forced the bike it would slow it down, and you could see that happening by watching the tach. I used to try different lines and watch the tach., to see how fast the line was. On one line the tach. might get up to 10,500, but on a different line it might only get to 10,000 by the same point on the banking, so the second line was not so good. I also used to try just crawling up onto the tank and letting the bike go where it wanted to, up or down the bank. If it was going for the outside I just let it go. Up on the tank it would be more stable because I had more weight on the front wheel and I could let my bike go as loose as possible and not hold a death grip on it. But I kept watching the tach., to see which way made the bike go fastest.

At Daytona you do a lot of slipstreaming and use it to pass, either on the high or the low side. It depends which is most convenient and which will frighten the life out of them.

When I had the old piston-ported engine in the Grands Prix I had to draft. At Ricard, the last year I rode the bike, I could hang in behind the Suzukis, Randy and Marco, but I couldn't pass them. I had the last corner onto the back straight wired. Coming through the double right they used to smoke me, but they never worked out that the next left onto the back straight was about five times more important. They would rush in and have to shut the gas while I was building my speed, which was vital on the old piston port.

I had to let them get away through those two rights, even though I could have stuck with them. It might seem bad to lose ground where I didn't have to, but I knew that I would make it all up and more, going through the next left. The year I beat them there it was funny, because Yamaha knew that Suzuki had a speed advantage and that it was unlikely we would win. When I won they could not believe it. We had a big party after the race, where they thanked me for winning when they thought they were really up against it.

There were a few places at Ricard where my bike was definitely working better than theirs. I was quicker through the right-hander at the end of the back straight, and through the left going onto it. The piston port was a funny engine and I didn't realise the advantages it had until I tried to ride a disc valver. At Ricard the circuit is split into two halves, the two ends separated by two straights. I could just put one, two or three bike lengths between us round each end and then they would come back down the straights, so I had to hang on to their slipstream. I kept working at it, though, getting further away round the corners until they must've got held up by traffic and they didn't get past me again. Once that happened it was enough of a break, and they couldn't catch up. It just goes to show that even if you do not have a bike that's fast enough to blast away down the straight you can still race with someone on a quicker machine, because you can use the draft to hang on to them – up to a point anyway.

One of the things to remember at a track like Paul Ricard is that getting the power to the ground is more important than straight line top speed.

Most of the time people going to Ricard think that the back straight is so long they have to have a lot of top speed, but what they also have to realise is that there are a lot of corners. They are not banked corners and they don't give the best traction, because the surface is so hard on tyres that they don't work that well. If you don't have a real fast bike you have to look at your advantages, and my advantage was that I could get the power to the ground. I could go around the corners, and get out of the corners faster; they were having trouble getting out of the corner and onto the back straight so I was making speed on them there, and I could draft them. We didn't have the peaky power to give us the top speed but the flatter power was an advantage in itself, and we made that work for us.

It is not always the fastest bike that wins the race. Even if you go to the line fourth or fifth fastest after practice, that does not mean that everything is over – it is not time to give up. There are other things to be taken into account: this is a race and it is different from practice. You have to think that the other riders might have problems, they might not have your conditioning, your concentration, and you have to exploit your advantages. At that time at Ricard my concentration was at a peak and I knew that I just had to keep pushing and pushing, and it worked.

There were races when the draft didn't work for me, like the British Grand Prix when Jack Middelburg beat me. I was setting it up to pass him

Special circuits like Daytona require special racecraft on the banking as Roberts demonstrates on the 750 square four in '83 when he won from new team mate Eddie Lawson after both had tyre worries on the ultra-powerful machines: low on the tank, as perfectly streamlined as possible and putting the minimum of pressure on the bars.

on the run up to Woodcote. I would come faster out of the fifth-gear left-hander up the hill. No one could go through there as fast as I could, not that day at least. I was just waiting for the last lap because I knew if I led into Woodcote he might come inside and just take us both out. I gave him some distance and ran up behind. Everything was right except that there were some slower riders there, Franco Uncini and someone else, both on private bikes. What I did not anticipate was him catching their draft. That took him away from me and past them. I caught them and had to weave through them, just at the last second going into Woodcote. I didn't try to pass him then because I didn't want to take the risk of doing something silly at the last corner. I had anticipated using his slipstream to get by but, as it turned out, he was able to use someone else's draft to get the advantage. I had planned on picking up speed on him but I didn't – it was him who picked up speed.

When I raced Sheene there it worked out better. That was in '79, the time my gearbox blew an oil seal coming to the line and I got oil all over my gloves trying to wipe it off the wheels and tyres before the start. Kel just pushed the seal back in and we had to hope it was going to stay there for the race. I knew that there was no way that he could go through that left-hander with me, as we had been together all the race. I had two plans, either to let him lead up the hill and then pass him before Woodcote, or to make a break for it on the last lap. What happened was that when I came out of the first corner on the last lap I glanced behind, and he wasn't right on my tail. I thought, 'This is it, don't wait around', and I went for it, not looking back again. What I expected him to do was to draft me up to Woodcote, but you can see on the film of the race that he could not get through that last left-hander fast enough.

I could go through there flat out, even in '83 on the V four, if the gearing and everything was dead right. I could just roll it off in fifth and then get on the gas again, going from white line to white line. I would be hooking sixth over the hill. It makes a lot of difference. I think there are other riders who get in there just as fast but then have to roll the throttle because they are not quite certain where they are going. If I ever rolled the throttle the rev counter would not come up to the point where I shifted into sixth till about two hundred yards later.

It wasn't something that I could do every lap at will, and I didn't do it very often. It depended on the wind and a lot of other things. Maybe three laps was the maximum number of times I could do it. It required a lot of strength, timing and concentration. I did not view it as high risk and I could do it if I needed to get a lead; then I would ease it back down below flat out and save that concentration till I needed it, maybe at the end of the race. That is why lap times vary during the race, of course, and they may pick up at the end if it's a close thing. You are saving your concentration until the end.

Using other riders is something that can be very useful, if you do it right. The best place is going into a chicane or tight 'S' bend. If you can go in and just slip under one or two slower riders, and the guy behind can't, then you will be able to break away. I found that I could not concentrate 120 per cent for more than three laps at a time, so I used to wait for a chance like that. Use back-markers to make a break, go for it at 120 per cent for three laps, and hope to build a lead.

There are circuits like Monza where races are often won or lost with slipstreaming.
Top: Coming out of the Parabolica, Mamola leads McElnea, Sarron, Taira and Haslam.
Middle: McElnea hunts for Mamola's slipstream while Taira is tucked right in behind Sarron but Haslam is too far astern to benefit.
Bottom: Mamola is towing McElnea even though he is slightly to one side so that he can see the corner approach. Sarron obscures Taira from view in similar fashion. The Mamola/McElnea battle was not in fact resolved by slipstreaming but by Mamola coming off worse when both men tried to occupy the same piece of track at the same time on the last lap: not recommended racecraft.

You have to plan a race. Coming up to the corner you have to be computing what you are going to do. You are riding your race at a certain lap speed and your brain should be working so well that everything seems real slow and you can see the slow guys ahead as you lead the race, with two or three guys behind. You have to be thinking about where they are going to be when you arrive at the corner, and if you can you get past them just in time.

You can make a break for it on your own, but if you are circulating around the lap record anyway, then any little help is going to be a big advantage. If you are the first guy to go past the slower riders, then you have the advantage. The two you are catching are riding their own race, not doing anything silly, then you go by on the brakes and that shakes them up. The guys behind you can't be sure what they are going to do because they are startled, and almost bound to move off line a foot or two as you go past.

It can depend what bike you are on. In '83, as many times as I dived past tail-enders first, Freddie's three-cylinder was so manoeuvrable it never seemed to slow him down at all. If he went past first I had real trouble, because my four would not change line. I just couldn't put it on to the same piece of road fast enough.

One last-lap plan I used a few times was to set an early brake marker and use that throughout the race – until the last lap, where I would brake at the proper place, yards later. That is what I did to Freddie in Sweden. It worked, but I guess I underestimated him and the lengths he was prepared to go to to finish in front.

Racing close to other riders is something that keeps you on your toes. You've got to make sure that if the other guy falls, you don't go with him, so you have to watch out for things going wrong. The year that Middelburg beat me at Silverstone, Crosby crashed early on. He was leading going down the Hangar straight and I anticipated his falling. He used to ride with his elbows sticking out, which meant you could see his elbow go up as he went to take a big handful of throttle. We were all in there and I didn't feel we were going too fast but we were not very far into the corner, pretty early to get on the gas, when I saw the elbow go up as though he was saying, 'OK, so long, I'm out of here guys.' I thought, 'Hell, if I did that I'd crash, and if he gets away with it he'll be gone and no one will catch him.' Then I saw the smoke coming off the tyre and I realised he was history. I picked the bike up but I made a determined effort not to look at him. I just looked inside, at the corner, and then I got it down again just before I ran out of room.

Then things started happening behind me, as Sheene and Lucchinelli went down. The temptation is to look at the crashing rider. You pick the bike up and go with him off the track. It is an easy thing to do but fatal. You have to look at the corner, not at him: if you look at him it startles you and you crash as well. I made that mistake the next year, when Graham Wood crashed in front of me. I picked the bike up when I saw him and touched the wet kerb. It's easy to do. I have been in many races where guys have crashed in front, but as long as you look for that inside line and go for it you will get through OK.

You should then take it easy for a lap or so, because oil might have caused the crash, or some fuel or water could have been dropped in the accident. I knew it wasn't oil that had caused Crosby's accident because I saw him accelerate so early and Randy, who was on his team, had told me Crosby was running a weird gearbox that day, using second in that corner, and it was making revs real early in the turn.

Sometimes being right behind the crashing bike can be a disadvantage, other times being five or six bikes back can be a disadvantage, because if several bikes go down you can see it all happening and it is hard to decide how to pick your way through. When Uncini fell off in front of Gardner and me in Assen I just shut off, because as I came round the corner he was spinning and rolling. I slowed to see which way he was going to go before I made my move. I then picked the inside line and he saw me do that and started to move to the outside of the track. Gardner was behind me, though, and had no chance of seeing what Uncini was doing, so when I started to go to the right Gardner went to the left. There was no way Gardner could miss him.

Of course there is no point in riding at 100 per cent if you don't have to, so you should know where you are in the race and what is going on. You have to know where you are in the race. When I was Grand Prix racing we were always thinking about winning, so the most important thing was how many seconds I was in front. But of course it didn't always work out like that. Some races we were more interested in one particular guy, like Sheene in '78 and '79, for instance. I would want to know where he was and what he was doing. If I was second but he was back in fifth there was no sense in me trying to win the race. If I had to take a bunch of chances to win the race then it would not be worth it. But if I didn't know where he was, I might take unnecessary chances to win. If I could win riding at only 95 per cent, fine. If it was the end of the year and I had a points lead then there would be no sense in running at 100 per cent when I didn't need to.

I never bothered with lap times. There are riders around that do like to be given lap times but not me. I never asked for a lap time in race or practice. I felt that if I was riding my motor cycle good I didn't need to know how fast I was going.

I remember the first time I rode in the Suzuka Eight Hours. I went out and tried to put in a fast time and take pole away from Gardner. I waited until the last few minutes to go out, so he wouldn't be able to go out again. I gave it 100 per cent concentration. I came down the straight, having just got sideways a bit coming into one corner and had overshot a couple of feet at the apex on the previous lap. I was thinking, 'This is it, next lap and I'll sort out that corner', but as I came down the straight the damn Japanese held out a pit board and I thought, 'What the hell was that?' It had all these numbers on it and I pulled in and asked them what it was all about. They said, 'You have record, you have record.' I said to hell with that. They said, 'We didn't want you to go any faster.' I said, 'You worry about yourself and I'll worry about how fast I am going.'

After ten years of never getting a pit board suddenly there it was and it freaked me right out, blew my concentration, and I pulled in. I wasn't used to it, we had never used them, but Kel wasn't there. The only time we bothered with a board in practice was if I had to run a motor in and

had to do fourteen miserable laps – then they would tell me how many I had done.

It was funny when we first went to Europe because I only had one bike. I was breaking it in almost every week so Kel would hang out the board: 14 laps, then 10, 9, 8 . . . 1, and then he would hang a sign 'GO' and I would light out. Everyone would say, 'Hell! There he is just riding around until you hang out a sign that says "GO" and then he sets the fastest time.' That used to crack them all up and no one realised I was running engines in. People would say to Kel, 'So he doesn't go for it until you say so. How do you know when it is time for him to go for it?' That was fun.

Randy used to be given lap times in practice, but I just think it's bullshit. What are you going to do if you get a good time, pull in? You are

The Yugoslav Grand Prix at Rijeka in 1983 and Eddie Lawson is given the message: 'Six laps to go and Kenny is seventeen seconds behind.' The hidden message was: 'Slow down and let Roberts past.' Kenny had been last off the line and, while Spencer cruised to a comfortable win,

out there and you should be riding as hard as you can in practice, trying to put in the best time you possibly can, otherwise you are not testing the bike or yourself. If someone went faster than I did then there was not a hell of a lot I could do about it. I didn't need to check my times to know if I was trying or not. I knew if I wasn't trying and that wasn't often, because I didn't like getting beat.

When Freddie and I were racing nose to tail for the lead in '83, then there was no point in getting a pit board about him. The board would just say +14, or whatever, to the guy in third and the number of laps to go. The number of laps to go would be all I was looking for. That year I would be lying second, chasing Freddie, and Kel might give me −3 on the board. Now either I have a problem or the guy is just blowing me off. Then he would give me −4 and later, −5, −6, −7. I am thinking, 'To hell with that, I know I am getting blown off. What about the guy behind?', and I would go past the pits pointing behind. Then I would get '10 laps' and I'd know how much of the race there was left. I knew I was getting blown off, so quit rubbing it in. I used to get a laps to go board every five laps and then 10, 9, 8, as a countdown to the end.

You have to know where you are at. We screwed up sometimes. The first time I went to Imola for the 200-miler I didn't get a lap board to say I was in second place. I had a ten-second lead going into the pit stop but Ago had a faster pit stop than me and I was just cruising round. I saw him at the end and he was in front of me, but by then it was too late. I'd thought he was behind.

Good pit signals are essential. You should get signals so that you don't have to wonder where the other guy is. Don't look behind you, that is the general rule. There are points, like rounding a hairpin, where it is possible to glance over your shoulder, but most of the time it is so dangerous it is just not worth it. It is like looking behind you going down the freeway. You can do it once or twice, even three or four times, and nothing will happen. But sooner or later you are not going to get away with it and the consequences are so bad it is not worth any of the times you looked over your shoulder and were lucky.

You might make it through your career, looking behind and getting away with it, but I have seen kids run into the outside wall at a dirt track race looking behind and they never knew what hit them. They never knew what mistake they made to kill them that day. I have looked back at places where I thought it was safe enough, but you see some riders look back every lap and sometimes three times a lap. We know that Barry Sheene had looked behind him when he hit that bike on the track at Silverstone, because he said so afterwards. That's the sort of thing that can happen. When I took his helmet off I thought he was dead, and if I ever needed a lesson on what not to do, that was it.

Roberts charged through the field but could not get the extra two points for third unless Lawson slowed. Team orders are against FIM rules but when championships are at stake the rider with the chance of the title usually takes precedence. On this occasion, Lawson did not take the hint.

Chapter 7

Tyres

Since I have spent a lot of time testing tyres I suppose that the feedback I was giving about the tyres was good or they would not have been using me. You can learn a lot when you are testing, about the bike, the track and the tyres, but you have to be pretty good before you start or you will not be consistent enough to do reliable tyre testing.

Testing tyres is a good thing to do for many reasons. If you are good at it then you will put in a lot of test miles, you will get plenty of time on the bike, and you will improve your riding by pushing the tyres 100 per cent. If you are not good at it no one will use you for tyre testing and you will miss out on the track time. There is no substitute for track time, and that track time must mean riding pretty close to 100 per cent if you are going to learn anything about the tyres or improve your riding.

It certainly does sharpen you up, especially before the start of the season, if you can get time testing tyres. It makes a big difference because you are pushing the motor cycle 100 per cent and then you can pick out two or three corners on the race track where you can push it 110 per cent. That is where the feedback comes from: you have to pick the corners on the track that will easily give you the feedback you need.

I have done a lot of testing at Laguna Seca and there Turn Seven is a downhill left and that makes it real easy to sort out what the front tyre is doing. Any time that you have a downhill corner the front tyre takes care of perhaps 70 per cent of the turn. At an uphill corner it might only be about 15 per cent because as soon as you are off the brakes you are on the throttle, and as soon as the engine is above idle the front tyre does not really come into it. It is the back tyre that is doing all the work and taking the load. On the downhill turn the front end is loaded much harder, and the steeper the gradient the more load there is on it. Even when you get on the gas and the engine comes off idle it is hard to take all the load off the front. While you are trying to turn through the corner, with the load on for a long time, is when the front is going to push and you have to be paying 100 per cent attention to it or you can lose the front right there.

So, say you are using that Turn Seven at Laguna, you have to ride fast enough to get confidence in the front tyre and then you can start pushing it harder at that point, to see where the limit is for that tyre. You are trying harder and working your confidence up to the point where suddenly the tyre does push and then you have got to ease off. You have gone quicker and quicker, just gradually, until it slid; and because you didn't go in way over your head you have saved it and you know where the limit of that tyre is. Then you put a new front tyre on and start working on that one,

Tyre testing at Laguna Seca in January. Not all riders can summon the enthusiasm or determination to push to the limit when the racing season seems a long way off. It is not the easiest thing to do when there is no one to compete against but unless you do push the tyres to the limit you can learn little.

getting your confidence back in exactly the same way, just gradually working at that one corner, taking no notice of the back tyre because that is some standard old thing that you know, and anyway you are not pushing it that hard. Round the rest of the track you will be taking note of how the front tyre feels through some other corners, how it feels over the bumps, how light it makes the bike steer, but you are only really pushing to the limit, using all your skill and concentration, on that one corner and you push and push until you find the limit. Unless you can work up to the limit with every tyre you are not testing it, and you won't be able to tell the tyre engineer what he needs to know to do his job.

The good guys can do it within a few laps. They can say, well, this one pushes, that one doesn't. You can't do that on every corner, you cannot use 120 per cent concentration at every point on the race track. You have to cruise on some of the corners and just pick a couple of corners to push it hard. You don't ride round and round looking for a good lap time. You will do that towards the end of the test session, when you have got front and back tyres that you think are the answer. Then you will want to run off a series of fast laps to see how both tyres stand up to lap after lap at high speed – but that only comes when you have weeded out the bad stuff.

My tyre testing started with Goodyear and that was because I was probably the fastest racer they had when I was starting my road racing career. I did a lot of testing on the 350 and was probably one of the first guys to use the slick tyre. I was working with Bill Robinson and John Smith in Goodyear's early days, trying to make a slick work. To my mind they were the answer, but no one else wanted to test them because they didn't work at first. When they were first tried they caused some very bad chattering problems. I worked with Goodyear, testing and testing, to try and find out why they chattered. I wanted to use the slick because I could already feel it gave more traction and was just about impossible to slide, but you never could push it that far because it chattered so bad. It was just about unridable, it didn't matter what compound we used.

We thought that the chattering might be caused by the tyre not having a tread pattern, so the Goodyear guys started to cut tread into it, to see how much it needed to get rid of the problem. We ended up cutting a full tread pattern in those tyres and they still pattered. We had one cut just like a triangular Dunlop, which was the best tyre at the time, and it was still no good. Then we realised that it wasn't the rubber or the tread pattern.

I felt that it had to be something else, so I went into the truck and grabbed the used Dunlop to have a good look at it. As soon as I got hold of it the casing felt so soft that I thought this had to be the answer: the casing construction and the lack of flex in the tyre were causing the chattering.

We were at Talladega at the time and John Smith went back to the factory and got to work on a batch of new tyres with a much more flexible casing contruction. He flew tyres in to do the next race at Laguna and they looked like bicycle tyres they were so soft. They blew out to a good shape once they had air in them, though, and I just smoked everybody in the race. That was in '73, I believe, and after that it was all slicks and there was a lot of testing to be done. As it was a new thing the engineers could try a load of different compounds, constructions and profiles. We also started getting much more powerful bikes and instead of just having to put tyres on a 350 twin we soon had the 700 Yamaha to ride, and that had twice the engine capacity and twice as many cylinders. It was not only a lot faster than the old 350 but a lot heavier and at places like Daytona tyres became a real problem.

I remember going to Daytona in '74 and testing forty-eight rear tyres in three days, trying to find something that would cope with the power and hold together. When you are testing that many tyres there has to be some sort of system. You have to have the base-line tyres that you have used before and that are known to work. The engineer knows what to expect from them and you know that you can use those tyres to set competitive times at various tracks. The idea then is to try other tyres and compare them to the base-line tyres, to find something that works better.

The tyre engineer in charge of the test doesn't tell you exactly what he is doing, what tyres he is putting on, because the idea is for you to tell him what you feel, not for him to tell you what to expect. Every so often he will slide in a tyre that you have already tried, to compare with the other tyre and see if what you are saying makes sense. He is not trying to catch you out: he has to be sure that you are riding consistently and that what you are telling him is true and not affected by your getting faster or slower as the day goes on. They have a good idea what to expect, because if they have a group of, say, five tyres with the same construction but different compounds they will expect a certain feedback. If what you say about a tyre does not make sense they will carry on with testing other tyres, but they will slide that particular tyre back into the programme a little later to get a second opinion.

I could always say, 'Well, I have tested this tyre before. It feels just like the tyre I rode on eight tyres ago, because it did this or felt like this.' The guys just used to smile. Obviously they thought I was very good at it. It is possible to remember what tyres feel like for a long time. For instance, we had a compound one time with Goodyear, it was A29 and I remember I hated it. What that rear tyre was good for was that it had fairly decent traction and lasted a long time. It had a little bit of grease in the compound and that meant that when you worked it hard, instead of tearing the rubber off, it would just grease up. That tyre hung around, and some of the other guys used it and loved it, but I hated it. My style is to slide the rear end, which pushed the tyre that much harder, increased the temperature and the grease would come out that much more. They would stick that tyre on, because they wanted it to last the race, and every time I'd hate it after three laps because of the drift going into the corners; the drift coming out didn't bother me, but this tyre would go sideways on me going in.

There are circuits that are better for tyre testing than Laguna – almost anywhere that is hot, Rijeka in Yugoslavia, Malaysia, Misano in Italy – depending on what you want to test. You can make a good start at Laguna but in the winter it is not easy to tell how the tyre is going to go off, because it is not hot enough. I could always tell, though, and I have raced at Laguna so often and tested there so much that I have a good insight into how things should go. But it is not a very demanding place on tyres; if you

Saving front tyre wear at Laguna Seca, '79. A World Champion demonstrating his oneness with the machine.

really wanted to test the life of a rear tyre it would have to be a hot abrasive track like Malaysia.

It makes no difference whether you are testing compound or construction, you are either going to feel an effect on the performance of the bike or you are not. You feel it through the handlebars and the seat. You have to have that sort of feeling to push it to the edge. Some riders have it, some don't. Some riders can do good, thorough tyre testing and some can't – and there are a lot more that can't. It's a big problem in the motor cycle business. With cars it is easy to test tyres; if you are on a motor cycle and push it over the edge and fall down then it is not easy to get back on and do it all over again. I've tested car tyres and it's no problem to spin out once, then put new tyres on and go straight out again. Bike racing is not that easy. You have to push until you get down to a lap time that you are happy testing at and then, because the weather heats up or you get used to the track, things change. If you put a tyre on that you hate you can find that you are going two seconds a lap quicker because the wind has dropped, or the temperature has warmed up, or you are just trying harder. You have to test tyres close to your race time, close enough to full speed to feel the tyres sliding around.

The rest of the bike does not have to be dead right. If the suspension is a little off that does not matter, as long as you don't change things in the middle of the test. You do have to have the suspension good enough for the bike to be ridable, of course, because unless you can push it to the edge you are not going to learn anything. But consistency is more important than perfect suspension.

You have to look at both the stopwatch and your own feeling, and for me the feeling is more important. If I had two tyres that were close but one was a little faster on the stopwatch and the other felt better I would run them back to back at the end of the test. With three tyres I would run them hard and instead of doing five laps do, say, ten and see which one panned out. Usually I am pretty certain which one tyre out of the bunch is the one I want to use.

Radar guns are a waste of time, the stopwatch is much more accurate. When you are testing, consistency is the key. You pick out a brake marker for the corner, you know where you gas it in the corner. Then you feel the traction and you pick out the tyre that really hooks up and you realise that you can get the power on earlier. So you pull that tyre off and leave it to the end of the test, then you can try it again and really hammer it.

By the end of the day the tyre engineers should have enough information to develop the next set of tyres. There's construction testing and compound testing as well as tyres of different profiles and sizes. They will have an idea that this family or line of tyres is the best one. They may have families each with the same construction. If they have constructions A,B and C then they might have five As, five Bs and five Cs in different compounds. Out of them the tyre engineers will see which construction is working and put it together with the best compound in the tyre size and profile that suits the machine.

At the end of the day what you are looking for is a better combination for your motor cycle. You are testing tyres, but you need a combination that works with your motor cycle. That does not always mean the tyre that gives the ultimate grip, but the one that suits you and the motor cycle best, and allows you to get round the track quicker. Because bikes have different power characteristics, weight distribution and steering geometry the tyre profile, construction and compound that is good for one will probably not be good for another.

Testing a tyre on a Yamaha, for example, will produce a best tyre that may be, and in fact usually is, totally different from the tyre that is best on the Honda or Suzuki. When I am testing I don't care which tyre has been proved to be best on the Honda or the Suzuki, because what I am looking for is the tyre that is best for my machine. I am looking for that bonus, that little edge that I am going to get from the right combination of tyres for my machine, and picking the tyre and adjusting the suspension so that the two work together.

Whether you are racing or testing, warming up the tyres does not take long. It depends how long the track is, but at a GP-length circuit you only have to allow one lap. The tyre should then be good for about 70 per cent and after one more lap you can nail it at 100 per cent. So when you are tyre testing you only have to do one careful lap and then you can work into full speed. You should only need four or five laps in all to test the tyre initially. The good tyres you give longer. You push them harder and see how they hold up.

You don't just have to accept the tyre as it is. If you think that a certain tyre shows promise, but it feels a bit harsh, you can ask the tyre engineer to lower the pressure a little and give that a try. On the other hand, I used to have to run more pressure in my front tyres than Eddie and the other guys in '83, when I was using Dunlops. I ran a harder construction front because I forced the front tyre into the turns harder. Going into the chicanes I was forcing the front tyre so hard with the handlebars that it would take a whole bunch of that abuse and then give. The lighter construction that everyone else liked would take the force and then spring back. I needed the firmer construction that was more positive and did not spring back.

On a fast corner, turning in real hard, I could make the front tyre start to tuck under. A place where that effect was important was Imola and the fast left-hand sweeper after the pits. You can put a great deal of force on a front tyre there, pulling on the left-hand bar going in to make the bike lie down. I always pushed the front tyre hard going into the corner, that is my style, to go from straight up to on my side in the shortest possible distance – and that means forcing the front tyre to take a lot of turning load. I want to feel the front tyre start to push instead of just riding around, because unless you are pushing the front then you are not riding as fast as you can. I set the bike so that it does just start to push and then I know I am using the traction to the maximum.

At certain corners you will use a lot of handlebar pressure, at others none at all. I don't push the front end real hard in corners where the consequences of going in too hot are bad – either where there is no run-off and you are going to get hurt, or where you will run out of road coming out. The only way I will make up time with that sort of corner is on the brakes, or accelerating out of the turn. I don't want to go into the corner any faster than the rest of the guys because I take more of a chance of

*Dunlop America's racing tyre genius Jim Allen
working with Peter Ingley fitting tyres for the Lucky
Strike Team. Budgets often do not run to teams of
fitters at test sessions and the engineers must do
the work themselves.*

running off the road coming out. My theory has always been, why try to make up time in a corner where you have more to lose? The idea in racing is not to fall down, and I think I only fell off once in a Grand Prix, in England when a guy crashed in front of me. That was in six years of Grand Prix racing so it is not a bad average. I don't know of too many people who can say that and have won as many races as I did. Don't take chances where there is such an obvious risk of falling down.

I don't feel that radial construction has meant that you can lap a great deal faster, but you can keep up those lap times through the race. In that respect I think tyres have come a long way, because they do last a lot longer. Five or so years ago you could go to some tracks and after a few laps the rear tyre was junk, it just started sliding around and there was nothing you could do with it. Now you can muster some more steam late on in the race. The last time I rode at Laguna Seca was with a radial on the rear and I went my fastest at the end with ease, just saying to myself, 'Man, I can't believe how good that tyre is.'

There have been times when tyres have not been so good. There was one year in Finland where things got a bit strange. It was a dangerous race track in any case, and we had a real tyre problem there. Goodyear had built a new tyre because they wanted to run softer compounds, but they were going to pull out of this race because they did not have a tyre that would stand the heat and the straight line speed. So Tim Miller, Goodyear's GP technician, designed a bigger tyre and that year we were running a real heavy duty construction, to give us traction coming out of the corners where we were losing it. The tyre he made replaced the 3.75 size; it was wider but flatter. The trouble was we went straight from the upright to the side section: the lean-over patch became the acceleration patch. Tim then built another tyre that was a similar profile to the old tyre but a little larger all round.

The night before the race Miller had to make a decision. I had never run any tyres in practice that would last the race. They kept blistering along the centre line because they were so heavy, with too much rubber in the middle. Kel said, 'Well, why don't we just cut some rubber off the middle?' So we took this real big tyre, which was the one that ran the coolest and stood the best chance of lasting, although it did not steer as well as the little tyres I was used to, and went to cut some rubber off it. Kel rigged up a swing arm and put the wheel in it, with the tyre fitted, and as Miller spun the tyre Kel machined the rubber off with the tyre-cutting tool you usually use for cutting grooves to make rain tyres. It was like a tyre lathe. Kel took about a quarter of an inch out of the middle of the tyre, which put a big flat in it. It was a pretty wild thing to do and I don't think most people would have believed we would try something like that – but we had to try something.

Miller warned me that it was dangerous, and he had no idea if it would work, but it was either that or not race. He told me to pull in if I felt any kind of vibration. It handled like hell and when I arrived at the first corner I could not turn the bike at all. I looked like Randy Mamola, I was hanging off so much. I missed that corner so often that there was the normal line and then there was Kenny's line that went straight on, way past the point you should turn. It didn't help that the road had a heavy camber. Until I passed the crown of the road the bike would not lean at all. I was trying to ride the bike down each straight, saying to myself, 'Is that a vibration? What was that?' In the end the bike quit and the tyre had just started to come apart. That happened to me twice: in '78 there was rubber flying off the rear tyre and the ignition quit.

So much of racing is about people, and as I said at the beginning the tyre engineers are as important as anyone. Before his move to Pirelli, Peter Ingley was one of the Dunlop engineers who worked most closely with our team. His experience, design ability and advice were vital. I chose to go with Dunlop after Goodyear pulled out and since then I've done a lot of tyre development with him. No one knows more about racing tyres, testing and developing them.

Helping Mamola out with the tyre development while Baldwin was injured, Roberts takes a ride on the Lucky Strike Yamaha while Peter Ingley, then working for Dunlop, prepares to benefit from his feedback. Though entered for the race, Roberts only tested in practice but still impressed many other competitors with his speed and style.

Peter Ingley

' The tyre designer relies a great deal on the riders he is working with. We have tests we can run in our laboratories but they do not always mean exactly the same thing when it comes to performance on the track. The rider can either confirm or contradict what we have found in the laboratory. Even if he contradicts it, that is a lesson in itself. The rider is so important because not only does he tell us what he needs in terms of performance improvement, but also if he does not feel comfortable he cannot go fast. It is a two-way thing, though, because there comes a point when the rider has to believe us when we say that he can push a certain tyre a little harder on the brakes going into the corner, or he should be able to get the power on a little earlier. It is hard for a rider to believe something that means risking his neck, but at Grand Prix level you have to work up to a point of mutual trust.

We came to that point with Randy Mamola at the Austrian Grand Prix in 1987. It was his fifth Grand Prix riding with our tyres on the Yamaha, and I knew from other work we had done that he was not pushing the front radial as hard as it could go. There is a lot of time to be made up at the Salzburgring, going into the long right-hander at the paddock end of the circuit, and as we were not getting anywhere in practice I told Randy that he should be braking all the way into the corner. It is not every rider who I would say that to, but I have known Randy long enough and I know what he is capable of. Sure enough, in that Saturday afternoon session he began braking deep into the corner and his times came down until he was second fastest.

Randy is one of those riders who can really tell you what is happening. He is probably one of the best tyre testers, and he has a remarkable ability to sense even the smallest changes we might have made to a tyre. One example of that was the way he picked up the minutest difference between tyres during practice for the Portuguese Grand Prix at Jarama. Even he can go astray, though, and at the beginning of the year we had problems at the Spanish Grand Prix at Jerez. We ended the meeting there with the riders saying that everything we had was wrong. It was fairly obvious from their comments that they were slightly confused about their feedback from the tyres, so I decided to scrap all the information or misinformation we had received there and start again at the German Grand Prix. When we later used some of the tyres that had been regarded as useless at Jerez, the riders liked them and used them.

Tyre design is not easy because there are an infinite number of possibilities for any tyre. The changes you can make to compound, construction and profile, which all affect each other, mean that you will never end up with a tyre that is perfect. All that you can hope to do is provide a rider with a tyre that is better than he needs at that moment; but when you make a tyre that will cope with the power of the engine he will just push it harder, so that he demands more from the front tyre. Then you have to start working on that again.

The rider has to be able to concentrate on what he is doing when he is riding. We expect some feedback, not only when he is testing specific tyres but also during normal practice because there is no time to test with every bike at every track. The rider has to have the concentration to tell you what is happening.

We do not expect or want the rider to come in and say that the construction needs changing or the compound is no good. That is not his job and he does not need to know that much about tyre design. What we want the rider to tell us is what the machine is doing at various points of the circuit. We need him to describe his feelings, so that we can sort out what that means in terms of tyre design.

The tyres do not work on their own and I often have discussions with suspension engineers and frame designers, because our work overlaps. What they do affects me, and so on. What the rider thinks is a tyre problem may be a suspension problem, or the other way round, and when the suspension is changed it affects the way the tyre works, and vice versa.

Every racer, from the start of his career, should be interested in the tyres he races on. Anyone should soon start to see how a choice of tyre size, for example, affects the way the machine steers. It is a mistake to think that you will go faster simply by using the biggest tyres that will fit the machine and, in all honesty, until a rider gets to Grand Prix level he should find little to complain about from his tyres. Whatever he rides he should be able to get a recommended tyre that suits his needs. The standard racing tyres as sold over the counter will be more than good enough. Even at Grand Prix level there are very few riders who are genuinely better than their tyres. There are many who voice an opinion but only a handful who can actually push the product to the limit, and most should be well satisfied with the tyres that are available to everyone. **,**

Chapter 8

Riding in the rain

Riding in the rain freaks some guys out but it shouldn't, because the same things apply that do in the dry. You have to feel what the bike is doing. Most of the time you fall down in the rain because when you try to go fast you lose the front end. The front end slipping away is the typical wet weather accident. You cannot really feel the front end push in the wet – there is not enough feedback – and by the time you feel it, it is usually too late to save it. It is safer to slide the back end, just like riding in the dry. You can feel the back end come round and that is adjustable with the throttle. If you give it a big handful of throttle then you are expecting it to spin and you can shut it off.

I remember the first time I rode in the rain. It was the second time we went to England and we'd often been told to watch out if it rained. There was this one British guy, Dave Croxford, who was always telling us that if it rained we'd be in trouble. He raced a twin-cylinder Norton and always reckoned that he would be able to get the power to the ground while we would be spinning out everywhere. His theory was OK. The Norton could get the power to the ground and it handled well, but the only thing wrong with that was that the four-cylinder two strokes could blast past up the straight, then just put the brakes on and stop, without having to try and go faster round the corners.

It helped that Goodyear had built some rain tyres for motor cycles. They had already developed rain tyres for Formula One car racing and John Smith, who was my engineer at the time, just decided to put that pattern on a motor cycle tyre in a good cold weather compound that would still last a long time in case it dried out. The tyres were all hand cut when the first batch was made, and we took them to England for the Match Races. Sure enough, that year it did rain. Very few of the Americans had ever ridden in the rain. They had made a rule in America that there would be no racing in the rain because, since we had all started using slicks, not many tyre companies sold rain tyres.

So all the British knew was that we didn't race in the rain. Croxford came over to the American pit area and made a big thing of it, rubbing his hands together and saying in this weird cockney accent, 'Cumon Yanks, get your wet tyres on.' Then he looked at our rain tyres and started cracking up laughing.

Christian Sarron, seen leading Rob McElnea during practice for the 1988 Japanese Grand Prix, excels in the wet. He won the 1985 West German Grand Prix at Hockenheim in similar conditions but Roberts points out that relying on the front end as he does is risky even in the dry.

We went to the startline and they gave us a couple of laps of practice to get used to the wet. What I did was go round real slow and use the rear tyre to feel for how much traction there was. I had no idea how much grip the rear tyres were going to give, so I just kept testing, giving it a little more power and a little more, a little earlier in the turn every time, till it started to slide.

When they dropped the flag we just split. I think there were two English riders in the top eight, maybe Sheene and Grant. As for Croxford, I remember coming around to the second and third corner, the right and left off the back straight, and seeing the flags out meaning that there was someone off. I thought, 'Oh man, I hope that is not one of the American guys', because of the team points. Then I saw it was Croxford, taking off his helmet and wiping off some mud. After the race, which I won, I went

to his pit calling out, 'Croxford, hey Croxford!' He just turned around and said, 'Shudup Yank!' But he was always a good guy for a joke.

After that Goodyear tyres were like gold, and the riders who didn't have them just said, 'Well, anyone can win on Goodyear rain tyres.' It wasn't that at all. Sure, the tyres were good, but we were used to trying out the grip. Racing dirt track, where the amount of grip changes every time you go out on the track, as the surface dries out or gets more cut up, you just have to feel for it.

Riding in the wet is something at which you don't get a lot of practice. It depends where you do your riding, of course, but the Americans never have. If it rained in practice in Europe and I did not think there was a strong chance it would rain in the race, then I didn't go out. I don't believe in practising like mad in the rain. I don't think that World Championships are won in the wet.

But I do think that if you are an American who has grown up racing dirt track then your style will suit riding in the wet. There is a big difference between all the American styles of riding and a European who is supposed to be very good in the wet, like Christian Sarron. Christian does go well in the wet, but anyone that uses the front end hard like Christian and the other Europeans do is bound to have a lot of crashes. When he doesn't crash everyone seems to think that he goes very well. I don't agree. Anyone who goes very well in the wet, with a European-type style, takes a lot of chances. The thing to do is to figure out a way of going fast without pushing the front end so hard. Use the back, so that when it slides you have a chance to control it.

The difference between the normal European style and the American way of riding is pretty obvious when you take a look at it. I saw that when Kel came to race in America. He had the basic European style when he first came over from riding in the Grands Prix in Europe. The first time I realised how I differed from Kel was at a 125-mile race in Ontario. The track had a very fast, smooth surface, and one section with three corners all in one, so that you had to make one big sweeper out of them. We had the same motor cycles that Kel had prepared, and the same tyres.

We raced that entire race nose to tail. Kel had a different gearbox, and right at the end he got a bit of a lead on me and beat me. I was a first-year expert and had barely done fifteen road races, maybe less. Kel was going to beat me no matter what, because he had so much experience. He knew what he was going to do if it came down to the last lap. I was just glad to be racing with him; finishing second would make me plenty happy because I was racing with someone who had already been very good and won the World Championship. I respected him and looked up to him. He had taught me a lot.

In the winner's circle I noticed that his front tyre was bald, all the tread was gone; my front tyre was only half worn out, but my rear tyre was bald. Kel said to me, 'Look, you must be riding that thing wrong or something.' I thought to myself, 'Wow, that is a big difference', and I started putting things together. I really didn't know much about road racing then. In dirt track racing we just used the rear tyres and this made me realise that I was doing the same thing with the road racer.

It was the same at the 1984 250 race in Kyalami, South Africa, when

Battling with Gregg Hansford in the rain on the 250s. Roberts always enjoyed racing with the Australian but, as he explains, he once made a classic mistake in the wet, misjudging an overtaking possibility which took him off the narrow dry line.

Wayne Rainey was riding in his first GP. He and Martin Wimmer had the same bike and the same tyres, and they raced together for the whole race, which was wet. Wayne's back tyre was bald at the end and the front tyre was like new. On Wimmer's bike it was the other way round. It's just the American style and the way we learn to ride a motor cycle. And it suits riding in the rain.

If you go fast in the rain you take the chance of falling down more than you would in the dry, because in the dry things are more predictable. You know from experience how fast you can go into a turn. In the wet you cannot be that sure. Some Europeans are better than others in the wet. Like Sheene: he had enough feel and technique that if it rained at a race track he liked he could get on with it. He was never as bad on the front end as Christian, he was smarter and he didn't like falling down, it wasn't his thing.

When you are riding in the wet you have to watch your style and also the lines that you choose. Don't take risks. Trying to find the dry or the driest line is more important than the right line, because you have to find the line that gives the most grip. That will be the dry line if there is one, but if it is all wet there will still be some places that are more slippery than others. A lot of race tracks often have cars on them and most of the time they lay a lot of rubber and oil where they put their outside tyre. Sometimes you have to stay inside and sometimes outside this, but it is almost always a slippery patch that is well worth staying away from.

You have to watch and feel all the time. What may be a good line at the beginning of the race may run through a three-inch puddle by halfway, so you have to change your line. You have to look for the least amount of water, and keep clear of the rubber and oil, but conditions will be changing all the time.

You have to look where you are going and feel for grip with your rear tyre. Any time that the front starts to push you're looking at disaster, and you have to do something different. In the rain I always go a little more cautiously, a little slower into the corner, and give it more gas coming out. That way I can find the lines that are giving traction and discover how much grip there is available. This also heats up my back tyre more, which gives more grip. The only problem is that when it starts to dry out you can be in trouble with that rear tyre. If the track is drying out you want to keep the tyres as cool as possible, because heat really kills these soft compound tyres. It is worth looking for the wet patches on the straights where you don't need the grip and running through them. That will get some water on the tyre and keep the temperature down a little.

You shouldn't hang off the bike as much in the wet. You don't need the weight transference. You should soften up the suspension, front and rear, depending on the bike and the rider's preference. Some people like a high ride height in the wet, some low. I'm not sure it makes a great deal of difference. I always took half a turn off the shock pre-load and lowered the front by 5mm on the spring pre-load. That gave me a little more feel, and we also backed off the damping. It all makes the suspension move a little easier, which helps you know what is going on, and you are not braking or accelerating as hard so you do not use as much travel. This means that the initial suspension is softer, so that when you go rushing into a corner it will absorb some of the load. When you go into a turn the energy has to go somewhere: if the suspension can absorb it then it won't be transmitted to the tyres. If you lean over too much, too much energy will be put into the tyre and it will slide away.

Like the suspension, the gearing needs changing for the wet too, because you are not going to get out of a corner fast enough to reach the same top speed. It varies from track to track, but usually it works out that you have to put two teeth on the back sprocket and you will be something like seven seconds a lap slower on a GP circuit. If there is a very long straight you might have to have taller gearing and you can still get a high top speed. You might also need to change the internal ratios. What we used to do in that situation was to put the larger rear sprocket on, but also put in a taller sixth gear. Normally two teeth gives you about the right gearing for the corners, and the straight as well.

You should never go at 100 per cent in the rain. I never did. I only raced in a couple of wet Grands Prix. It is too easy to fall down and you don't get any points for crashing. If you look at all the races in a season not many of them will be wet, so when it does rain it is better to take things easy and just go for a few points.

Braking is not a problem as long as you make sure that, at high speed, the front end is loaded before you get on the brakes hard. You have to touch the brakes, bring the front end down a little bit and make sure there is pressure on the tyre or you could lock it up at high speed. The wind is going into the fairing and that makes the front end light. You can lock it up real easy.

Aquaplaning should be no problem. What you have to watch out for is that you *don't* try to *do* anything when it aquaplanes. The bike will move three or four feet sideways when you are travelling in a straight line, but as long as you don't try to do anything with the front it will come back.

Your touch should always be lighter in the wet. Everything you do should be lighter. You should be putting no pressure into the bars because none can come back from the tyres. The lighter you are with everything, the more you will feel. And don't go forcing the bike into a corner, like you would in the dry, because the tyres just don't give enough grip to let you do it.

From the riding point of view it is easier in the wet — easier on the muscles, you consume less energy. The only thing you might use more of is concentration, because you need to concentrate over the full distance of the race. I might use 110 per cent concentration and effort for some of the time on a dry race track. In the wet I might only be using, say, 80 per cent, but I am applying that *all the time* because you just can't afford to forget where you are at.

Stay away from white lines and painted kerbs, they will have you down instantly. That is what happened to me at Silverstone in '82. I didn't get the bike started and I was last off the line. It had rained but it was drying out and we were on slicks. The kerbs were still wet and Graham Wood, one of the English riders, fell in front of me at the first corner. I picked the bike up to miss him and when I tried to put it down again I had run out of room: I touched the painted kerb and it was gone.

When it has been very cold and wet I have used plastic face shields

Rain riding demands even more than usual throttle control as a slide so quickly gets out of control. Here Jacques Cornu leads Rosa de la Puig during the 1987 French Grand Prix at Le Mans. Cornu has a wealth of road racing experience and had plenty of opportunity to ride in the rain while he was Endurance Champion but

taped to the fairing to keep the rain and the cold air off my hands. It is the cold air that really hurts. It depends on the fairing that you are using, but protection can make a difference to the amount of water getting onto your gloves. That soon starts to numb the feeling in your fingers. I use plastic dishwashing gloves to keep my hands from getting wet. I've tried them both inside and outside the gloves; either will work, depending on the fit of the gloves.

On the visor you have to apply 'Fog-free' on the inside to stop it misting up, and it is very important that you breathe out of the bottom of your mouth. Push your top lip over your bottom lip and breathe the air out downwards, because no matter what sort of visor you have it will probably mist up if you don't. Some riders, like Randy, always seem to have a

problem with visors fogging in the rain. I never breathed that hard in the rain because I used less physical strength than in the dry, and I made a conscious effort to breathe out through the bottom of the helmet. Different people have different problems, depending on the shape of their face and the way their helmet fits.

The thing that always upset me in the rain was having to wear a rain suit. If the rain suit is not just right it can really mess you up. If it is too tight it restricts your movement and then it is impossible to feel comfortable and concentrate on riding, because every time you try to move the suit stops you. Even though you do not move around as much in the rain it is very important that you can move freely. Of course, a loose rain suit is no good either, because it will billow around all over the place. You have to have a good, well-made rain suit that fits well but has enough give to allow you to move. On my feet I used to wear plastic bags inside my boots but over my socks.

Even with a good clear visor, following other riders or passing slower men can be a problem because of the spray. You have to stay as clear of other bikes as possible. The other thing to watch out for, if there is a great amount of water lying on the track, can be the wash from other machines. Stay clear of the waves coming off the other guys' tyres, because it can make the water deeper than it would have been.

Choosing what tyres to use in the wet is obviously very important. I have come to the conclusion that you should either be on rain tyres or slicks and you can forget intermediates. The intermediate does nothing for you. If it dries out you won't be able to go as fast as if you had a slick on, and just because it has a few grooves in it does not mean you will be able to lean over in the wet.

The last race I rode in the rain on a 500 was in Japan and I had to make the choice between a slick and a treaded tyre. There was water on the circuit, with some dry spots. The Japanese engineer, Maekawa, said that I should use intermediates because there was water running across the track in places. I said 'No way' because if it dried out the intermediates would soon be wasted. Mike was determined that I should at least use an intermediate on the front, for safety, but the more he tried to talk me out of using slicks the more determined I was. As we started the race Eddie was still not sure what he should do, but decided that if I had slicks on that is what he would run.

The race started and I was following Asami, who had intermediates front and back. He pulled away from me, maybe five bike lengths, coming up this hill where we went from first gear to fourth gear through a long, sweeping right-hand corner. He could do that there because the initial grip of my slick was not as good as his intermediate; the slick had not built up enough heat to get the compound working. The track started to dry out, though, and I made the decision to split once I felt there was enough traction. Eddie caught and passed him at the end of the race as well.

When the race track is drying out you have to watch for the dry line which develops on the racing line. It is always narrowest at the apex of a turn. The mistake that most people make in the wet is the same one they make in the dry: they do not look far enough ahead. If you try to stay on that line, looking just in front of you, then you will miss it. You have to look way ahead and not worry about the line, then you will be on it. If you think about the line, and try to stay on it, you will go too slow and will probably wander off it.

Passing people in that situation is just the same for me as in the dry. You have to think about it beforehand and plan it. I don't like rushing past on the inside, going into the corner. With the dry line you can just slow down a little more going into the turn, then drive past and around on the way out. If you do have to go onto the damp, doing your passing on the way out, you will be controlling any slide you might have on the throttle. There will probably be enough dry road to use anyway, because the dry line is always wider coming out of the turn than it is in the middle. If you misjudge going into the corner, passing someone in the wet, then you have no room to correct it as you will be arriving at the narrowest part of the dry patch all wrong.

It is easy enough, sitting back in my chair at home, to describe what I think is the right and the wrong way of doing things. That certainly doesn't mean I always did it right on the race track. I remember one particular goof-up at the Imola 200-miler, during one of my trips to Europe. The bike had blown up in the first heat, so for the second leg I had to start at the back of the grid. I pumped myself up to go for it right off the start, even though it had been raining and the track was only just drying. I went charging through the field and I think it was the second or third lap when I was catching Hansford, who was fourth. I thought to myself that really I should wait for a clear chance, but my bike was faster than his and it was just too tempting as we came to the end of the back straight up to the chicane. I whipped out of the slipstream at the end of the straight, off the dry line and onto the wet, to go up the inside. It wasn't such a bright move because Gregg was the best braker on the track and there was I trying to outbrake him while he was in the dry and I was hung out there in the wet. I realised as soon as I whipped out that I was in big trouble and I ended up running into the back of the Kawasaki as he flicked it into the chicane. He didn't even know what had happened — he thought he had hit the kerb. Of course I fell off and ended up sitting on the wall watching the race, drinking wine with some of the spectators.

Chapter 9

Machine design, development and testing

You have this bike sitting in pit road and its only restriction is you. I went through periods where I was better than the motor cycle, in my opinion, but at the end of the day it is up to you to try and get the motor cycle changed. Through my Grand Prix career I struggled with that and it was not until 1983 that we finally put together a motor cycle that was positive and adjustable. The shock readout made sense, and you could tell someone what it was doing and they could fix it. We could adjust that motor cycle and go faster.

There were other years when it wouldn't have mattered if you'd put a stick where the shock was – it would have made no difference. The frame flexed so bad that nothing in the whole world would make it work. It made you feel like an idiot, because nothing you did improved it.

In '83, when they finally made the bike stiff from steering head to swinging arm pivot, that made all the difference. We had the right linkage system in the rear. Up to then we'd always had trouble because we never did have a monoshock that worked. It was only when Ohlins got involved, and designed the shocks, and changed the whole suspension layout, that the rear suspension started to work. From the day they started working with us my life changed. I actually started to enjoy riding the bike and sorting out the rear suspension, because what was going on made sense.

I have spent a lot of time working with the Japanese since I started Grand Prix racing. I would go to Japan at the end of the season, around September, for a race that they run at that time of year, and we would have meetings over several days to discuss what we felt we should do for the coming season. What was the next step? Should we move the engine forward, make it lower or whatever? What should the steering angle be? Where should the centre of gravity be? Sometimes I felt that they were asking me questions because they wanted to make the bike the way I wanted it; but other times I think they just wanted to see what I had to say. Either way it did not bother me that much, because I realised that they needed the input.

There were things that I asked them to make, so that we could test, that never turned up. There were other things that I only mentioned casually that would get made. So I was never sure what their reaction to what I said would be. The engineers have a pretty good idea of what they want out of you, of what they think is wrong with the bike, from their own testing

by the factory test riders. A lot of times you don't know what the Japanese test riders have said about a bike. There are a lot of Grand Prix riders that don't have much respect for the factory testers, because they are not very fast when it comes to a race. I have respect for any rider, especially when he can tell me that the steering head angle is wrong. I never claimed to be a great tester myself. I just did what I could to help get a bike that would win the World Championship.

I was not a stickler on bike preparation. I didn't care if it ran a little dirty down low, but I did care if the throttle didn't move easily, because that affected the way I controlled it. I just wanted to go faster than anyone else, and I concentrated on the big issues. The test riders did a brilliant job of cleaning up all the smaller stuff that still goes into making a good motor cycle.

They would bring the bike to Laguna in February, after it had been tested perhaps a couple of times in Japan. I would usually have three days on it there and make suggestions. Then they would make changes and bring it to the Grands Prix.

At the test they would bring with them the parts that they thought would be best to try. They would bring carbs, pipes, perhaps different cylinders, crankcases and ignitions. I would start off riding what they thought was the best combination; then we would try other things. More often than not they were right in what they thought was the best, plus they had their own ideas on what else they wanted to try first. But since I talked the loudest we usually tried things in the order I thought would be best. Kel played a big part in it too because, being a rider, he knew what made sense to try and what didn't, so he would tell them what he thought. He was a real big help, especially at the beginning. That doesn't mean Kel and I always agreed, because a lot of the time we would clash head-on, but I always won because I had to ride the bike. We had a lot of disagreements about things like riding styles, but we put that aside and did the job of getting the bike sorted out and going racing. We both had a lot of respect for each other and what each of us could do, but we could argue like hell. Sometimes we did five or six hundred miles of testing and even after that there would be more when we got into the season.

I would keep requesting stuff – a different chassis with the engine further forward, a lower or a shorter gas tank – and they would arrive at various points through the year. There were times when we had urgent mid-season testing. As I said before, I once flew to England to test at Silverstone for one afternoon and then flew home, just because we had to test something.

The story really started in 1977, when it looked fairly certain that I was going to go to Europe for the next season. I had heard from Stevie Baker and I talked to his mechanic Bob Work about the problems they had had Grand Prix racing with the Yamaha. I formed my ideas from what Stevie said: he could not brake hard because the back end was hopping all over the place. He felt that if they just threw the monoshock away and replaced it with a set of twin shocks then things would be a whole lot better.

So I had a mental picture of what the bike was like and I had been working a bit already with Kel, moving the engine around in a standard 750 chassis. I felt that the 500 probably had quite a bit of front engine weight,

Roberts getting some ideas on machine development way back in 1974 during his first Grand Prix visit. The machine he is photographing at Assen is Giacomo Agostini's 500 Yamaha. Despite winning this race, Ago could only manage fourth place in the Championship which was headed by the MVs of Phil Read and Gianfranco Bonera, but he took the title for Yamaha in '75.

possibly more than it needed. I went to Japan with a mental picture of the swing arm pivot being too high. I'd been racing at Paul Ricard on the 750 when they had the 500 there for Stevie, to put in some track time, and I'd told Kel then that I thought the swing arm pivot looked too high.

What that meant was that the bike would tend to have a very abrupt loss and gain of traction. Either there was nothing, or a lot, and it would dance around coming through the corner. When I went to Japan at the end of '77 I rode one of Stevie's bikes and I told them I thought the swing arm was too high. I also went over bump dampening with them, and what I thought was wrong with it. I felt they were trying to cover too much with bump dampening and not enough spring. From speaking to Stevie and watching films of him racing in Europe, and then riding the bike myself, that was what I felt was wrong with it.

It's a funny story. It was the first time I had worked with Maekawa, who would be my engineer on the 500. I had met Mike but never worked with him before, and I told him I wanted to take a shock apart. That surprised him but he took me to a back room and we took one apart. I had seen shocks apart before in America, and I had goofed plenty of them up by drilling holes in them, making orifices to try to make them work better. I used to do that to Kel – take three shocks apart and wreck them – and

he would get mad at me, but I knew I was learning. This one had a back orifice next to the bladder with three settings: low, medium and hard. I said to Mike, 'This is the bump dampening, right?' He said, 'Yes.' So I took that out and threw it in the trash can, just leaving a big hole. Then I said, 'Put it back together and we'll give it a go.' Mike said, 'But you can't do that.' When I asked why not he said, 'You just can't.' So I told him I would put it back together and asked him to go to the motocross department and get me the heaviest spring they had. He did and I cut the spring to fit.

We went to the test track the next day and put the shock on. He was saying, 'Please don't test that shock', but I was determined to try it without any dampening at all. It needed a harder spring still, but after I had ridden it the test rider went out and said it worked. It wasn't right, and sure we needed some bump dampening, but it was the only way I could get my point across and it did make them think.

In the meetings after a test session we always have a blackboard and I drew on the board a bump and how the wheel had to travel up this thing and over it. I told them how I felt it should work, and how the bike felt soft when I sat on it but felt hard out on the race track. It was not that things were real complicated then, but no one knew anything. I worked with the S & W shock guy, Tim Witham. He had shock dynos and we used them on the dirt trackers but it related to road racing as well. I knew what I wanted to do but the problem was to get it across to people I hardly knew.

When the new bikes were built for the start of the '78 season I tested them and thought they were good enough to race, better than Stevie's. No one ever tells you exactly what they have changed, though – the swinging arm pivot, the engine position – but whatever they'd done it was an improvement. The bump dampening had been changed too. We won the first three races in a row, but for the last five laps of each I had real trouble keeping the bike on the race track. The bike wasn't bad, there were problems, but not a whole bunch. The shock problems continued for the rest of my career, until we went away from the monoshock system.

The piston-port engine at that time did not make the bike easy to ride. For the first race, the Venezuelan Grand Prix, mine did not have an exhaust valve. Johnny Cecotto's did, and mine did by the second race, but it did not make a whole lot of difference. It didn't make the bike that much more flexible.

Stevie had said that the Yamaha had top speed over the Suzukis, but he could not get it out of the corners, or stop it, and that was still my impression when I came to ride it in the Grands Prix. What the piston-port engine did have, and no one realised it, including me at the time, was the pushing power. It could spin the rear tyre but it still pushed the bike forward, whereas the Suzuki would just spin the wheel and go nowhere.

The rotary-valve engines were very different from the Yamaha and everyone had different ideas about how and why they worked. Wil Hartog had the best way of describing it. He used to say that on the Suzuki you could come out of a corner with, say, 5000 on the tach. and you could open it wide and it would just come in real docile, until it hit the power band. Wil's problem was that it would sometimes come in earlier than he expected and spin him out.

I felt that the piston port suited my style better than the disc valver. I

could get on the power early and it wouldn't spin the wheel, it would be bogging from early on, say 6000 rpm. If you weren't approaching 10,000 by the time you got out to the kerb, then you were doing something wrong. It had to be up to about 10,000 to really spin the wheel but it would run at 6, though it was only making best power from 10 to 12. The thing that I noticed straight away, when they built me the rotary-valve engine, was that it did not have the sort of power that you use from 6000. It would just spin the rear wheel instead of driving the bike forward. The second bike was better, the one that Sheene and some of the others rode.

From '78 to '79 they increased the power, and then for '80 we had the same power but they made the bike lighter and went to the aluminium chassis. In '80 they did put on the reverse cylinders, midway through the year, and that allowed them to do a little more with the exhaust pipes and get a bit more acceleration out of it.

At one point with the piston port I asked them to move the engine down and a little bit further forward. They built me a bike with the engine about an inch lower. I had felt that I was not getting the bike down on its side fast enough, and I was slow going from left to right. With the engine lower I could get it down much faster. After I tested it at Laguna Seca and really liked it, that was the one they produced for the last year of the piston port.

When I wanted more power from the piston-port engine they kept telling me that they could not do more because it was a piston port. I said that if that was the case they should build something else. They set out to build a disc valver, and they wanted to build a V, but they were worried about the vibration. They needed to do a lot of testing so while they were working that out they built the square four, which I never liked. The power delivery was never what I wanted.

The first time I rode it was at the Austrian Grand Prix at the Salzburgring in '81, and I did about sixteen laps to break it in. All they had was one complete engine and a spare set of crankcases. After it was run in they said I could go for it, but there was no way it would run. I came back in and said there was something wrong, either it was running on three cylinders, or if it was running on four they had better put it in the crate and send it back to Japan.

They changed the carburation but it still would not run. They had this bike that was supposed to turn out about 150 bhp, and it was a pretty big engine because they had no idea what that much power would do to the transmission. They had really beefed up the transmission, because the old piston port only produced about 115 or 120 bhp; at least, no one at that time would tell us what the dyno readings were, but I guess that is all it produced from the way it went.

We raced the square four and it never got any better. It just didn't get any better. It had a funny sort of power delivery. It ran as though it was never going to take off and reminded me of an engine which had the transfer ports too high. Anyway, the shock spring broke in the race so that saved us the trouble of having to finish it.

We went to Hockenheim for the next weekend and I had a meeting with the Yamaha engineer, Doi, and Kel and Mike. I told them that I thought the transfer ports were too high. Doi said that was impossible. I said that it might be impossible but the bike would not accelerate and I reckoned the ports were the problem. He said that the factory would check it out and I replied, 'Hell, we have to race at the weekend.' Never mind waiting for the factory to check it out. I wanted Kel to machine the base of the cylinders. They threw a fit. We only had eight cylinders and two of them had seized in Austria, because they were trying to lean it out so much to make it run – not to mention that it had thrown me off.

It was a two-day argument and Doi would not take the responsibility for letting Kel do it. I said, 'Well, someone has to take the responsibility. I would take the responsibility.' But Doi said we couldn't, because if something happened in practice we would be out of the race. I told him that if we did not get the bike going we were as good as out of the race anyway, because I only raced to win.

There were some real intense meetings. As often as I would tell Kel to do it, Doi would tell him not to, until finally I just said, 'Kel, go and machine the cylinders.' Doi was still screaming 'No, no we must test it in Japan,' but it would have taken three days and been too late. When he walked into the truck Kel was working at it, the lathe was turning and bits of swarf and cylinder were flying everywhere. He just went red and walked out.

We won that race, we just smoked them. We discovered that the castings were way out, half a millimetre too high on the transfer ports, and we  won two races in a row.

The disc-valve engine was never as good as I'd hoped, though, because the sort of power it produced would just spin the rear wheel instead of driving the bike forward. It had a load more power than the piston port, but it could not put it to the ground as well. We had a lot of suspension and tyre problems, too. No tyre compound we tried was ever hard enough, because the bike was so heavy and it just spun the rear wheel all the time, and the rear suspension would go off. We just could not anticipate things race by race and predict what was going to happen.

At the end of '81 I saw the V four, but the first one of those they built was not right either. Because the square four had been so heavy they went to a great deal of trouble to make the new V light. The heaviest parts of any machine are the engine flywheels and they went to a lot of expense to have magnesium inserts made for the flywheels, to take up the volume for the minimum weight. The trouble was, when it was finished, it was light but I couldn't ride it.

It was like a light switch, either on or off. I think I had one of the best rides of my career on that bike at the Spanish GP in '82, because it was all over the place but we won. I had to ride it off the kerbs because the rear end would just light up and take off anyplace but where I wanted it to go.

I remember when we got to Monza the disc-valve V four was just not picking up from its gearchanges the way I wanted it to. We couldn't go any leaner on the carburation and there was a slight pause watching the needle on the tach. We had tried changing the carburation, and we tried different pipes, but we couldn't get rid of it. I came in after one session and said, 'Could it be possible that the engine is getting just a little too much fuel?' Kel said, 'I don't know, let's try something.' We had blank rotary valves so I suggested that we make them open at the same time but

*Developing a better
machine involves sifting
through problems with the
engineers, working out
what can be improved on
the bike as it stands and
what will have to change
on the next model.*

119

close a little earlier. The Japanese engineer, Abe, brought out the dyno charts and showed us that, according to them, what happened if you reduced the opening time was that it produced less power. I said I didn't care about the power because I was losing too much time down the long straights at Monza, when it didn't pick its revs up after the gear changes. He still didn't believe it would work, but we tried it. The hesitation was gone, the engine picked up its revs and from that point in the season we started to go better.

There were a lot of problems in '82 because of the sort of power the bike was putting out. It wasn't helped by the tyres. Dunlop had made some real wide tyres to cope with the increased power – they knew from '81 that the bikes were now producing so much power and so suddenly they had to do something to cope with it, and they expected the '82 engine to be even more powerful. They opted for putting more rubber on the road and at the first race in Argentina we had this nine-inch wide rear. We didn't have adjustable steering heads so we just had to jack the back end up and steepen the steering head, because I couldn't get the bike to go from left to right. That big tyre just totally dominated the front. We had the back set pretty high to steepen up the steering head to around 22 degrees. That was a pretty drastic measure to get the bike to turn in. Normally we ran 24 degrees, just the same as we have now.

I would say that tyres now dominate machine design, because of the amount of grip they give. Bigger tyres with more traction and lasting longer mean that the bike cannot be flicked on its side as easily, and that means that the tyres are not going to spin and turn through the corner as quick. As tyres have changed it has meant that the bikes have had to change to make use of them.

Of course, there are other things that affect the way the bike handles, such as the centre of gravity. I have a theory that if you take a line through the wheel axles the weight should be concentrated around it (see diagram). If you could get all of your weight on that line you are 100 per cent right. The area just above and below the line is about 80 per cent right, but getting to the limits of the silhouette up and down is only about 60 per cent right. If there is some weight at the bottom and some at the top it does not make it correct but it helps because it evens things out.

Ideally I would put all the weight on the centre line and I would put the petrol tank under the seat. That's where I have got it on the dirt tracker I am building now as an experiment. When I was racing dirt track full time, and riding the Yamaha, I always had a traction problem when racing against the Harleys. I could smoke everyone in the heats but by the time it came to the main race a lot of tracks would have one hard groove round the inside, on the pole, and outside was so loose there was no traction at all. I would get into the corner fine but, without traction, I was soon out by the fence in the loose stuff. It made good entertainment for the spectators but it was death as far as my chances of winning were concerned.

I remember asking one mechanic to go to the skindiving shop and buy some weights that I could strap on. I put fifteen pounds of lead weight under the seat, and I did that every time I got to those race tracks where I had a big problem with traction. I damn near won the race with the fifteen pounds of lead even though in practice with a good cushion (a wide

60%

80%

100%

80%

Weight distribution is a major influence on the handling of a motor cycle. As he explains on the left, Roberts believes that, in order to obtain the most favourable characteristics, designers should aim to concentrate as much weight as possible around a line running through the front and rear wheel axles.

line with even traction) I could hardly ride it. The next race I used it I won by half a mile. No one knows to this day that I had a fifteen-pound lead weight under the seat, but boy did it make an incredible difference. So I am a great believer that if you have got eight gallons of gas, let's put it somewhere where it's useful.

The trend has been towards smaller wheel sizes, but everything has pluses and minuses. Is the advantage of the extra traction you can get from a larger diameter tyre with its bigger footprint worth the extra effort it is going to require to steer the motor cycle? When looking at anything you have to think what the advantages and the disadvantages will be. Everyone went to sixteen-inch front wheels from eighteen but obviously there were problems and we have now come back to seventeen. Rear wheels also went from eighteen to sixteen and back to seventeen. Dunlop have even experimented with nineteen on the rear.

I prefer seventeen-inch front wheels myself. I never did like sixteens and only used them for one year, on the big rotary-valve V, and that was when we ran the special steering clamps that had the fork tubes running through at a two-degree angle to the steering head. The steering head was real steep and I wanted the wheel pushed further forward so it would roll over bumps. It worked, but it was funny going into corners. I could feel the front end push better than I could without it, and we had the big rear tyre on the back, so we had to do something to make it turn quicker.

I was never that happy with the way they worked, but there were other riders who could not use them at all. I remember Sheene coming up to me at the first Grand Prix in '82. We both had square fours, because the V did not arrive until Austria. He said to me, 'Why do you have those triple clamps with the funny angle?'

I said, 'I don't know.'

He said, 'You know – they don't work at all. I don't understand why you're using them.'

'Well, did it ever dawn on you that I ride different from the way you do?'

'What do you mean?'

'You ride steering with the front wheel and I ride steering with the back wheel.'

He looked at me and said, 'No, I suppose you're right.'

'That is why I can use the triple clamps and you can't.' He thought about it for a second and walked off. Well, I thought, there was the guy who was my big rival for four years and he didn't even know how I rode. It shocked me. Barry was right, it didn't work.... But I won that race, he came second. The bike wasn't right but with that big rear tyre I was pushing the front and I pushed it a lot. Those triple clamps gave me the feel I needed to push it and not crash. Sheene was right. We don't use offset clamps now. But in that particular case, in that race, I needed them.

Sheene was always baffled by what I did and I have to admit there were things I did just to screw him up. When we were both riding for Yamaha he would tell me that the gearbox I was using was no good and I would use it just because I figured I could beat him anyway and it would get him going. When I had the V four and he wanted it, I told Yamaha to give him one but they said they didn't have the parts. When he got it for Silverstone he said the steering was too steep and had it changed. It was too steep for him because he was running Michelins while I had Dunlops, and I needed it that way.

Sheene had that big crash in practice and put himself out for the rest of the season. I broke my finger on the first lap of the race, so Crosby got the chance to ride the V at the German Grand Prix. He took it to the track but never raced it. He tried it but said, 'No thanks!' I walked into the tent at Hockenheim and he shook my hand and said, 'You are the bravest f...ing rider I have ever met' – just because of the way that bike was. I knew it had problems but Graeme was used to riding with the front end and muscling the OW60 around, and there was no way he could ride it. You had to ride it on the throttle.

Of course it is not just the wheel size and the steering geometry that affects the way a bike works. The engine characteristics are very important as well. With the square four and the early Vs I was always saying that it was the type of power delivery that was giving us most of the problems. The bike was better in '83 but it didn't get reed valves until '84, when I had retired from the Grands Prix. That was a shame. All the time we had piston ports and rotary valves I wanted reed valves because they're so good for power delivery.

Finally someone at Yamaha came up with a reed-valve induction system to the crankcase. I remember the last race I rode Maekawa told me about the new motor, the crankcase reed induction. He said, 'I know it has taken us this long to get you what you want but you can't quit now, you have to use the new bike.' I asked him how the power was and he told me there was more. I said, 'How can that be, because you always told me that reed-valve engines could never give enough power?' It was a big disappointment, but I did get to ride the bike at the Match Races and at Laguna, so I know how good it was with the reed valves.

So I never did get quite what I wanted. It came too late, but that is the point: you have to try and if you can't get what you want you have to make the best of what you are given. You will often have to make the best of a bike that is far from perfect, because you are never going to be in the position of being handed a perfect bike. I often tried to get the factory to change the bike but it rarely happened.

One thing I found I've had to get used to, working with the Japanese, is that they will never tell you why they can't do something. They will only say, 'No, it can't be done', or they might say 'Maybe'. They build the bike, of course, but all the time I spent in meetings, drawing diagrams, etc., they would never tell me exactly what they had done. I would just get the new bike and have to figure out for myself what made it different from last year's. I am only now at the point where I can work that closely with them. It took a long time before they would even show me dyno charts, so that I could tell them what their motor was doing on the race track compared with what it showed on the dyno. They came around eventually, though, and now I am one of the few people who can walk into the race department at the factory. I got there because I didn't go blabbing my mouth off when they told me something, and I guess it has also helped that I stuck with Yamaha and did not jump around between the different teams.

When you are trying to get the best out of the bike you have to work with both the factory and your mechanics. Only the factory can actually get more power out of the engine, and make it better. All that Kel Carruthers or Mike Sinclair can do is modify the engine to suit the rider a little more. They might move the power around a little, say give you more at the top end, but for them to make it any better they would have to have a dyno and all the testing equipment to go with it. They are not going to say, 'Well, this cylinder is no good', because the pipe is tuned to the cylinder and so is the carburation and everything else. Sometimes Kel could make the engine run better by cleaning up the cylinder, by taking the rough edges off. The factory does not do that because they have to produce eight bikes and a load of cylinders. The factory doesn't mind the mechanics cleaning up the cylinders to make them run a little better, that is just basic blueprinting of the engine.

When we developed at a Grand Prix we worked with the Japanese; that incident at Hockenheim was a one-off. Kel would go to Japan and work on the dyno there, offering his expertise, but it is not possible to do real development work at the track. We could not go off on our own and do stuff. We all had to work together.

Of course, at the end of the season, they would go away with all of our ideas – things that I wanted, things that Kel suggested would be better – and they would build another bike. As I said, you never knew which ideas they had put into the new bike and they were also working on other problems I was not aware of, so when the new bike appeared it could be totally different, they might have changed just about everything. Often it was no good asking what gear we'd run last year at a certain track, because the internal gearing would be different, or what spring we ran on the rear, because the shock was different or the linkage had been changed. We were always experimenting.

It was not until '83 that I could get the information I needed to win races, except from Maekawa. He spoke good English and would tell me what I needed to know. I won all my Grands Prix with him. The other engineers had been told not to tell the riders about dyno charts or anything else. There were a couple of seasons when engineer Abe would come halfway through the season and I would stop winning. I had a lot of trouble with him not telling me what was going on.

I had the same problems with rear suspension. They would change things and I could never get to see a diagram of the suspension system, to see how it was supposed to work. I never got the answers I wanted until Ohlins came along. From that point it all changed. It was as different as night and day.

Yamaha decided that they wanted to hire some help from Ohlins in the motocross area and we got the same help. I could relate what I wanted to the Ohlins engineers. I could never relate to the Japanese because they always talked in terms of force. If the rear wheel hit a rock it was the rate it moved, how fast it moved its given distance was how much dampening force it had to have. I never used that. I didn't understand it and could not relate to it. I used a stroke, with bump dampening on the top and rebound on the bottom, from my work with S & W. As soon as I started working with Ohlins they began talking low speed, medium and high on bump and the same on rebound. I am not a shock engineer but I could say, 'I

The startline, when all the testing, development and machine preparation are put to the test. This is Silverstone 1980 and Roberts occupies pole position next to Marco Lucchinelli and Graziano Rossi on the Gallina Suzukis. Sheene is in tenth place but Randy Mamola won from fourth on the grid after a close battle with Roberts and Lucchinelli who both had tyre problems, Lucchinelli losing strips of rubber from the centre of his rear. It was the year of the reverse cylinder 500 but Roberts did not use it at Silverstone.

think this one needs a little less rebound high on top because in fast corners it is just tying me down a bit', and that meant something to them. The first guy I worked with was Mike Mills and it was like heaven. For the first time I could dial the motor cycle in and it would stay there. It was great in '83.

From that moment we started to get somewhere. I always had my own ideas about what we should do to improve the way the bike was handling, but the old monshocks overheated so fast they were never the same two laps running. With the monoshock we were always having to guess what the bike might be doing ten laps into the race when it was hot and the tyre was going off. When the Ohlins were fitted, and the rear linkage changed, we started to be able to work at it logically.

The first thing that happens with too much rebound is that the bike wobbles, because the back end is held down. The shock is pumping down: the faster you go the more compressed it gets. You can put different pistons in the shock to prevent it from pumping down and keep the ride height up. When you hit a bump at high speed and the back goes down and doesn't come back that is usually a middle to high speed dampening problem. You have to loosen that up so that the shock responds and comes back quicker.

If you have too much medium and low speed it doesn't come back at all, it stays down all the time. If you have too little it will stand up and bounce, and then wobble, because it puts too much load on the steering head. You cannot say precisely, 'Well it is doing that wrong, that is the problem, and we will do this to fix it.' Half the time you are taking an educated guess and if what you do is an improvement then you have gone in the right direction. If not then you try something else. A lot of things are happening when you ride at race speed and sometimes it is hard to tell precisely what is wrong.

If you don't have enough bump dampening the first thing you will notice going into the corner is that it will bump once, twice, and if it does it again it will take off all the way through the corner. Three bumps and it takes off. I managed to nail that down with the Ohlins guys and it made a big difference. I had been getting the idea of what was wrong with the Yamaha guys, but the Yamaha shock would change so much in five laps that it would never be right. Just when you would think you had it, it would go away again.

When you have juddering, pattering or weaving, and you think that the suspension is wrong, you have to have an open mind. We have even had tyres that were out of round. You have to consider all that sort of thing when you have a suspension problem. With the front suspension we had a pattering problem a lot of the time and when it came down to it the problem was out-of-round tyres. When we had round tyres we didn't have any pattering. We went to great lengths in 1981 to try and get the front suspension sorted out but the tyres were so bad it was hardly ever right. I remember that year at Silverstone the bike was just about unridable. We had gone to a lot of trouble to put gas pressure in the front forks and that sort of thing but it was down to the tyres: Goodyear were having some problems and the tyres were out of round. (For front suspension springing adjustment, see Chapter 4 on braking).

Roberts ponders the rear end of the OW70 at Imola with the 1983 Championship hanging in the balance. Kneeling are Ohlins man Lars Osth and Kel Carruthers while Dunlop's Peter Ingley leans on the seat.

Sorting out suspension adjustment and handling problems is not just a case of riding the bike. You can learn a lot from watching as well. You have to watch at a corner that you know is testing the bike. You might pick a downhill corner for front tyre problems, or a left and right that are close together to see who is having trouble with a bike that won't change direction quick enough. You have to study and see who is having a problem, then define what the problem is. I have always been able to learn from watching other riders, to pick out what is going on with their machine. I can see things that normal people would miss. I might focus on the front or back suspension and watch one particular thing.

Even looking at photographs can tell you a lot. I used to do that before I even went to a Grand Prix. I remember looking through *Motocourse* from the '77 season and seeing pictures of Sheene on the Suzuki. He had the gas-oil rear shocks that used gas pressure and no spring, and I told Kel that they would never work. I reckoned his swing arm was sagging too much and he was losing traction. I said, if he runs the bike like that we will smoke him. Kel didn't take too much notice then. I talked so much rubbish I was a pain in the ass.

The first time I sat on Sheene's bike was in the pits in Venezuela, at the first race in '78, and he had those shocks on then. Even just sitting on the bike I felt they were wrong. He won the race and my bike blew up so I got to watch a few laps. I noticed that the rear suspension was being compressed and the swing arm was going past the point where the sprockets and the pivot are in line. I felt that was no good. By the time we got to Spain the gas shocks were gone and the standard factory units were back with the springs.

You can also see what the rider is doing, if he looks too tense, too tight. I have watched so many racers for so long through my career, either from the track side or by following them, the good ones and the not so good. I have learned different lines from a lot of different people. Even some guys who you would not normally think of as fast can have something to teach you. At Grand Prix level they are all good and they may have found a fast line through one particular corner that has something to offer.

We use video a lot in our team. We like to study film of our riders and the opposition. It is so useful because you can go over and over it, and then the rider can see what is happening. If he can see what he is doing wrong, or what is happening with the bike, we can either sort out the rider or the bike or both. We can analyse what is wrong.

After making famous the black and yellow of Yamaha America, Roberts was turned out in the black, red and white Yamaha International colours for 1981. By the time the Championship reached Imatra for the Finnish Grand Prix, Marco Lucchinelli had a six-point lead and was determined to extend it. No one got close in practice or the race and Roberts slipped back in the closing stages to finish seventh as the casting holding part of the power-valve mechanism cracked.

Roberts cresting the rise before dropping through Laguna Seca's famous Corkscrew on one of his visits to the mid-season international meetings that helped make them so popular. The support Roberts and his fellow countrymen gave the event made it so strong that when the AMA squeezed out the 500s, Laguna Seca was in a position to run a Grand Prix.

Roberts leads Sheene at Misano. The OW61 V four Yamaha was launched at the Austrian Grand Prix and Roberts fought it from there to the end of the season. Sheene, like the rest of the Yamaha riders, used the square four OW60 until he had the chance to use the V four during practice at Silverstone. Misano was typical of the struggles Roberts had and he finished fourth ahead of Marco Lucchinelli who said, 'For me he is still absolutely number one. No one else could ride that machine. When you follow him it looks as though he should crash. Anyone else would but with Kenny you know that he knows what he's doing and he can still ride it fast.'

At home with some of the
trophies and mementoes.
The phone rings
continuously and the only
remedy is to change the
number at frequent
intervals. The fact that he
has retired from racing
has made him even busier
but the trophies are now
spread round a larger
house.

Heading for World Title number three on the OW48 Yamaha, Roberts rounds the tight left-hand hairpin at Jarama, scene of the Spanish Grand Prix. He won convincingly, leaving the Suzukis of Lucchinelli and Mamola well behind. This was the second of three wins with which he started the year.

The Italian Grand Prix at Monza in '83 was memorable for Roberts for the wrong reasons as first he ran off the track passing a back-marker – 'Brain fade', he said later – and then the Yamaha ran out of fuel rounding the final corner and would not make it to the flag.

Right: Tucked in behind the screen, trying to wring the last drop of speed from the Marlboro Yamaha at Monza in '83.

135

One of the highlights of 1981 was the three-way clash at Silverstone between Roberts, Randy Mamola and Jack Middelburg. Graeme Crosby had crashed on lap 3 at Stowe corner taking Barry Sheene and Marco Lucchinelli with him into the catch fences. For 18 laps Kork Ballington also ran at the front until a disc valve broke on the Kawasaki. Then, with 3 of the 28 laps still to go, Mamola's Suzuki seized momentarily and lost power, leaving Roberts to do battle with Middelburg to the flag. The Dutchman had the better run at two back-markers on the way into Woodcote and won, even though he did not realise he had passed them until he saw the replay on television.

Spencer led from the line
at Spa in '83 but Roberts
hunted him down and,
when the man from
Shreveport had abused the
front tyre so much that it
threatened to drop him on
the road, Roberts took over
the lead on lap 14 of the 20
and pulled out a 10-second
lead going onto the last
lap. It was 14 seconds at the
end, suitable revenge for
'82.

The 1983 Dutch TT at Assen
saw Roberts at his best,
scything his way through
the field from a poor start
to catch and pass the
Hondas that were always
fast away. Spencer led but
as his tyres faded he was
passed by both Roberts
and Honda team mate
Takazumi Katayama. On
the rostrum (above) both
Roberts and Spencer seem
happy with their day's
work.

The climax of the 1983 World Championship: Roberts tries to slow Spencer so that Marlboro Yamaha team mate Eddie Lawson can catch up in the final round of the series at Imola. Just winning was not good enough for Roberts, as he needed Spencer to finish third or lower. The Honda was too manoeuvrable though and every time Roberts tried to slow the pace down, Spencer would slip past.

Roberts did not enjoy riding in Giacomo Agostini's team. Disagreements with the Italian in '83 were part of the reason he started thinking about retiring, although he also needed to spend more time at home in California with his family.

The triple World Champion makes a point. When he speaks, people pay attention. He commands such respect that his opinion and advice are widely sought. He may have retired from racing but he will influence the sport through the Nineties.

Chapter 10

Machine preparation

Kenny Roberts, Lucky Strike team manager, with Wayne Rainey and engineer Mike Sinclair discussing tactics at the 1988 Japanese Grand Prix at Suzuka. Though no longer competing, King Kenny can still ride a Grand Prix 500 fast enough to give valuable input for machine and tyre development. He tested the Lucky Strike Yamaha at Laguna Seca (below left) at the beginning of 1987 and at Jarama before the start of the 1988 season.

My idea is to have a team that is going to develop and put a motor cycle on the race track that runs better than the rest of the bikes. I do not want a team where the only difference between us and the other teams is that one has the World Champion riding for them and the rest don't. We have people who can work on the bikes and develop better machines. They have to work with riders who will test and push the bikes to the limit. Mike Sinclair is in charge on the technical side of the team and I feel he is the best in the field.

Mike Sinclair

No one knows more about today's Grand Prix 500 engines than Mike. He's worked with Wil Hartog, Pat Hennen, Virginio Ferrari and Randy Mamola on the factory Suzukis, Mamola on the works NS500 and NSR500 Hondas, and Mamola, Mike Baldwin, Kevin Magee and Wayne Rainey on Yamahas. He has just as much to offer the club racer and privateer, having himself raced to the point of being 1972 New Zealand 250 champion, before concentrating on machine preparation. He first went to Europe to look after Stu Avant's RG500 Suzuki in 1976.

' Whether you are racing the latest factory 500 or an old TZ350 Yamaha, many of the basic principles of machine preparation are the same. Most importantly, as far as speed and getting the best out of the machine are concerned, you should spend most time on making the carburettors work properly. There is far more to be had there than in tuning cylinders, pipes or anything else.

It is easy to think the carbs are working well enough, but it is often incredible how much of a lap-time gain there is to be had by working at them. Even when you think they are right you have to keep on trying different ideas, because that is when you will find the needles that work better right off the bottom, or make the thing pull harder in the middle. It is very hard to tell, on a transient throttle, how well the bike is actually running. You can only really find that out by experimenting with different stuff and comparing the two.

You have to rely on rider feel for your experimentation all the time, because one of the big problems with dyno testing is that it tells you

145

nothing about transient throttle performance. You can try roll-on tests on a straight but if the rider is top class, like Randy, you can rely on him. Give a top Grand Prix rider a bike with better throttle response and it will show in his lap times. They are so consistent with their lap times that such an improvement will show up immediately. But you have to have a rider who is at that sort of level, where his lap times are consistent and he is not still learning the circuit or how to ride the bike.

It is a great temptation for guys who are starting racing to spend too much time blaming the bike and trying to improve lap times by radical tuning. They waste time playing with the bike when they should be concentrating on improving their riding and their mental approach. The carburation is well worth sorting out, even for the club rider, but *only* once he knows that he can go round his local track at a regular 51.2 seconds, lap after lap after lap. That's the time to start experimenting with the bike, and hopefully he will then find he can do 50.9 seconds, lap after lap. Then he will know that somewhere along the line he improved it. Often you cannot tell exactly where the improvement comes from, but the lap time starts to come down.

If you are to stand any chance of finding out what it is that makes the engine perform better, the bike go faster, then you have got to start keeping records right from the first day you go racing. You should have a barometer and a wet and dry thermometer, because atmospheric conditions play such a big part in carburation. You have to develop a feel for what alterations are going to be needed in the carburettors when the weather changes. You have to keep noting the readings on the barometer and the thermometers, keep noting them even when you seem to be wasting your time and it means nothing to you, because after a time you will start to see patterns.

A really good thing to use are dyno correction charts, in connection with the readings you are taking and the carburettor settings you will need to change. The charts will not give you absolute values for changes to the carburation. All they provide is a number but, depending on the weather, that number will be either bigger or smaller than one, and this will tell you which way the carburation should be changed. You will start to see patterns in the way that this figure alters as well. It is all part of building up a picture of what is happening in the engine as the weather changes. In general terms the higher the pressure the more oxygen there is in the air and the bigger jets you need. On the dyno correction chart you will see that the number for the conditions that day is perhaps 0.99 whereas yesterday it might have been 1.02.

The wet and dry thermometers indicate the amount of moisture in the air. If there is a big variation in the readings of the two, that, in conjunction with the air pressure, will usually produce a high dyno correction factor, meaning the engine will burn less fuel and the carburation needs to be weakened out. When the wet and dry temperatures are closer together there is a lot of water in the air, and it replaces a fair bit of oxygen, so you will need smaller jets. Often the main jet may not change at all. You might increase the size of the needle jet because, especially with the modern 500s, at most circuits the engine is not running at full potential for very long and you are more interested in the transient throttle condition than full bore.

You always have to pay attention to reading the plugs, to keep an eye on what is happening, particularly with small engines, although with our 500s what we are doing often has no effect on the plug reading because we are not talking about being five sizes out on the main jet but making changes to the mid-range carburation. All we really have to do with the plugs is keep them away from being white. Often we look at the plugs and it looks as though you could run them leaner but we don't bother because that last fraction of top-end carburation is not going to give a significant improvement, and it might do more harm to the transient carburation that you have been trying to get right and which is more important.

The vital thing is that you develop a feel for the way that the air pressure and the humidity affect the carburation, and you want to tie that to figures on paper, to develop as accurate patterns as you can. Once you have started to see patterns in the carburation, then you will begin to see what needs to be done with the engine itself, because a lot of these engines do not create the right sort of depressions, they are not drawing gas, not pumping the way that they should all through the rev range. When you can understand the full carburation picture you can see where the engine is working and where it isn't.

In our case, we get new motors each year and very often we can see straight off from the carburettor settings what is wrong inside the engine. We can see that there are not the sudden pressure changes, the depressions that you expect, so then we have got to start work and create them by making changes inside the engine.

You will know when you have succeeded from the sort of carb settings that you have got, as well as the lap times that the rider is getting. Usually all you are doing is changing the frequency of the shock waves in the ports, exhaust, inlet transfer. The cheapest, easiest and sometimes most effective thing to do is experiment with the inlet tract length. Anyone can make up a set of spacers to go between the carb and the cylinder, and experiment that way. Often adding bits in rather than taking bits out can be the answer, even in the ports. Everyone is into grinding away and making the ports bigger, but there are an awful lot of motors that go much better with smaller ports, because you need to get the gas speeds up through the ports.

Crankcase volumes and things like that might be changed, but only if the engine is miles out. Packing the crankcases only really applies if you are converting a road motor to racing, and even then if you raise the rpm far enough the crankcase often needs the volume anyway. There are lots of different theories about crankcase volumes. For example, Honda's primary ratios are much higher in their racing engines than the likes of Yamaha or Suzuki. There are a hundred different ways of getting to the same result.

No matter what you are dealing with – piston-ported engines, disc-valve engines, or now the crankcase induction engines – the principles are very much the same. The carburation is still the most important thing, but with the reeds, for example, they require more attention than the discs ever did. The reed valves themselves need more maintenance and there is obviously a lot to be gained with different reed-valve designs and materials.

The Marlboro Yamaha set-up for '83. The Carruthers motorhome is parked next to the track so that he does not have far to walk to work. As long as the mechanics are at work, so is he.

There is more to come, not only from reed-valve design but from two strokes in general. Hopefully they are the engines of the twenty-first century. There will be more variable porting, variable everything, crankcase volume, transfer port height, everything controlled electronically. Then the two stroke will be really economical. It will be fantastic for the two stroke when you can control a few of the parameters better than they are controlled now. All the technology exists already; we are just waiting for the Japanese to decide that it is worth using it.

It is not just the principle of carburation that holds true, right from club racing to the Grands Prix. The club racer should be preparing his complete bike just as well as the Grand Prix mechanic. The most important thing again is keeping records: most guys don't even bother. Learn to be a real good recorder, right from the first time you race. It doesn't matter what you are riding, production bike or anything, just so long as you get into the habit of keeping records. Temperatures, pressures, lap times, gearing, jetting, tyres – it should be a little experiment from the first day you get on a racing bike till you become World Champion.

The trouble is that most riders aren't like that. The only rider I have ever worked with who kept a notebook and wrote things down was Virginio Ferrari, although Wayne Gardner apparently does. It seems that in most cases the guys who get to the top only care about going fast round a piece of road. They don't care about the equipment like the mechanic does. Right from the start you either have to have someone behind you who is keeping the notes, like Kenny and Randy did, or you have to do it yourself until you get to the stage when someone takes over. That is why, right from the start, if you are going to concentrate on the riding you have got to get someone to help you, either your father or someone else who is interested. It's a very big part of it – morale, encouragement, everything. The rider's morale needs looking after – not mindless ego boosting – but the rider has to be aware of what he can do. There are a lot of people who spend their time subconsciously putting themselves down; others can see that they have a lot of qualities in their riding that are well worthwhile. It is easy to doubt yourself when you are racing motor cycles, and the self-doubters don't get there.

Whether it is the rider or the mechanic who is working on the machine, he should develop a systematic approach. When you are experienced you know more instinctively what to look for, but that only comes with time. How much work you have to do depends on how good the bike is and how well you know it. Our bikes are so good now that we often leave well alone and don't tear everything apart every time the bike is run. That is down to records again, though, and knowing when things will *need* looking at.

Every time the bike is run, though, you must spend time looking at it, cleaning it, looking over everything for cracks in the frame (which you hardly ever find). The big thing is to put in a lot of time *looking* at it. You should not be finishing your bike in half an hour and then going off to talk to your mates. You should be finishing the bike in half an hour and then sitting there for three hours looking at it, thinking about how to make it go better. There are a lot of mechanics who aren't like that, who

This is the 1983 OW70. Although there were teething troubles at first, the V four Yamahas have developed a tremendous reputation for reliability and the modern racing two stroke is certainly not the frail creature of years past.

just want to wander off talking. They should be spending their time on the bike. During the season that should be your whole focus of attention, you should be zeroed in on that bike.

It is so often up to the people working on the bike to make it go faster. We think of modifications, alter the bike, then the rider goes out and we see if he can go quicker. The riders get bored stiff with testing:

'We don't have to do more of this, do we?' You can get into fights with some of them about how much more testing they have to do. It is easy to get the rider so stale with testing that if you have a race the next weekend on the same track he can be right in the doldrums. So you are better off, at our level, doing the testing at a different track three weeks away from the meeting. Don't stay on at the same circuit and grind yourself to a standstill. It is different for the rider who is still learning and improving, who just needs to put more and more miles on himself and the bike. But our guys can get really close to their best after, say, fifteen laps – then you ask them to do another hundred laps of testing. They get pretty bored about it all.

One thing we lack is the time to go and see our bikes and the other teams out on the circuit. You can learn so much from watching and timing bikes through a section – that's why it is so good for us to have Kenny wandering round the track with a stopwatch. He can see what is happening, and he looks for exactly the same sort of thing that we would be looking for. The more information, the better. It is definitely a team operation.

The team is important, though most riders don't appreciate being in a team with another rider. There are those who will not use anything on their bike that they didn't think of for themselves, and they miss out on a lot. It is better to have two riders, because you can filter out possible rider peculiarities from the machine testing. But the problem of having two is that, unless you are very careful, one will always be short-changed simply because when you finally discover something that makes the bike better, in the fourth practice session, there is no time to change both machines for the race – so he doesn't get it until the next week. That is why the number two rider often doesn't do much business.

We are getting to the point where we can get rid of most of that, because we have worked so hard at it. I believe we can run two number one riders, but a big part of that is to get rid of any feeling of inferiority between the two teams of people working. We don't tend to have that because we often have all four guys working on one bike if something needs doing. There is no separation in our team.

All our mechanics are more than parts fitters. They all contribute ideas to making the bikes go quicker. That is not to say everyone is the same, for there are factories who prefer to employ parts fitters because they don't want interference. Yamaha, particularly, are a very liberal bunch of thinkers as far as ideas are concerned. They are by far the most open-minded of the lot. They haven't got engineering snobs in their company. **,**

Chapter 11

Physical training

Physical training is the key to success in many sports, but the sad thing about motor cycle racing is that many people do not see the importance of it.

The ideal is to be generally physically fit, not just strong on one thing. When I was Grand Prix racing full time my daily routine would be to run in the hills of a golf course near where I lived for three or four miles. I just hated running but I did it because I had to. I also played racket ball for about two hours: it's good for stretching the muscles that get tense from riding.

I used weights if I wanted to work on something specific, like building up my back, but I never used them to build up muscles in my arms. To do that I rode and rode on the dirt almost every day I could get on the bike, say an average of four times a week. During January and February it was every day, to build up for the start of the season. There is no weight training in the world that will do you as much good as riding a motocrosser all day. If you get a young rider who does not have a lot of upper body weight he might need a bit of weight training, but in general I don't take the idea of straight weight training very seriously.

By the time I hit Europe in '78 for a full season it was a breeze, because I had been used to racing dirt track in the States every weekend from April to November, and training or testing during the week. In Europe I was actually doing less work, less riding than I had been used to.

I never found GP racing tiring, it never wore me down. Eventually I started getting trouble with my right forearm. The muscle would pump up and I couldn't feel the throttle. I was still out there riding but I thought I was going to hurt myself because I could not feel what I was doing with the throttle. I trained so much that I actually made it worse. I couldn't understand it so eventually I went to see a surgeon. They ran an electric shock test through the nerve and found out that the energy was not being transmitted up the nerve. They fixed it with an operation in '85, but I had quit racing full time by then.

One of the reasons I stopped was that I didn't have time for all the training I thought I needed to do because of my arm. I felt I had to do more training, that I had to work harder because I was having a problem that I put down to lack of strength or endurance in my arm muscle. In fact that wasn't the case and because I did not get the right advice, I was probably just making it worse.

I never bored myself with the same training schedule every day. I varied it so that I would use different muscles and not get so fed up that I couldn't face it any more. Some days I would just go and play golf, because I wanted to get away altogether, get away from business and all the rest. I needed the break that day more than I needed the training.

153

There is no doubt that the modern 500 requires a great deal of strength from the rider. Roberts found the Yamaha harder work than Spencer did the NS500 triple in '83. Here they both fight for control leaving La Source hairpin at Spa.

There is one extra muscle that you need for throttle control and that can be built up by using a straight bar with a grip on each end. You have a weight on a piece of string wrapped round the bar and you wind it up and down. That soon works at your throttle muscle.

Doing so much exercise I never had to worry about dieting, though in '82 I got interested in diets and how what you ate affected your performance. Concentration is a question of diet, so what you eat is vital. That was one of the things I found when Randy started riding for me; he did not eat the right food. I have always liked vegetables and eaten fairly good food; for example, I found that Japanese cooking is some of the best that you can eat.

I never ate meat before I raced because it takes a long time to digest. The only meat I would have might be a small grilled fillet three days before an event. Fish is good and veal not too bad. If you eat a big steak before a race your body needs water to digest that steak, and if it is using water to do that instead of supplying the muscles then that is going to hurt your performance.

I would start my build-up to the race on Wednesday. I cut out airplane food and carried a bag of mixed nuts and fruit when I flew, because I travelled so much. I quit coke and that sort of thing because it has so much sugar in it. It takes your blood count way up but then it suddenly drops and that's no good for energy. From Wednesday onwards I would eat pasta, fruit and cheese. Sometimes I would eat two or three pasta dishes per meal, for carbohydrate loading (see p. 160). For breakfast I would have cheese and fruit.

It made a big difference in '83. I set most of my lap records at the end of the race, when the old biased tyres were long gone. I went faster at the end of a race than Freddie did in the first five laps. My bike was not that manoeuvrable and I needed my concentration right to the end of the race. My goal was to be able to race 100 per cent for the whole race.

As far as drinking goes, the best thing is mineral water and plenty of it. No alcohol — maybe a couple of beers on Sunday night if it was a good race. I don't think a beer now and then does that much harm, but I felt that if I had a beer a couple of days before a race I was cheating myself. It takes days to get the alcohol out of the body and I was out to give 100 per cent.

I learnt a lot about diet and training while I was racing, but I also made mistakes and suffered because I did not have good professional advice. You can waste time learning and it is best to see an expert from the start. That's why I refer my riders to Dean Miller.

Dean Miller

Dean runs a sports clinic in Walnut Creek, California, where he looks after and advises many top sportsmen and women.

❛ I have worked with Kenny, Roger de Coster, Georges Jobert and Brad Lacky, who I have done more individual work with than anyone because I travelled with him for three years while he was doing the motocross World Championships. Brad was the first motor cycle racer I worked with, and from that association came Kenny.

Kenny has always been the kind of person who has trained, and realised that training was important to his performance. He has always done a lot of riding, dirt track and motocross, so the riding side of the training was there.

He did some weights, sit-ups, etc. and he also approached it from a healthy standpoint. When he started to go to Japan in the early '70s he found he liked the food. He changed from the average American diet and adopted the rice and the pastas. He got into the high-tech. vegetable mixes and drank a lot of carrot juice, tomato juice, that sort of thing. He started to limit his meat intake and for a Californian to do that is quite something. So he took care of himself in that sort of respect.

I think he adapted much better to Europe than some of the other road racers and motocrossers who tried it, because he took his motorhome across and that, to a certain extent, made him independent. He could carry his own fruit and vegetables with him, and not have to worry where he was going to eat during the day while travelling across strange countries.

A lot of racers will not do that. They are stuck into the idea of eating three meals a day, eating in restaurants and getting steak and eggs. If you can't get them to change completely they have to be convinced to taper down on those sort of foods. I think that since I became involved with Brad Lacky and then Kenny, and one or two others like Jeff Spencer have been involved in training, things have changed a lot and motor cycle sport has become one of the most aware sports in America, as far as fitness and training are concerned.

Racers take better care of themselves than they ever have, more so

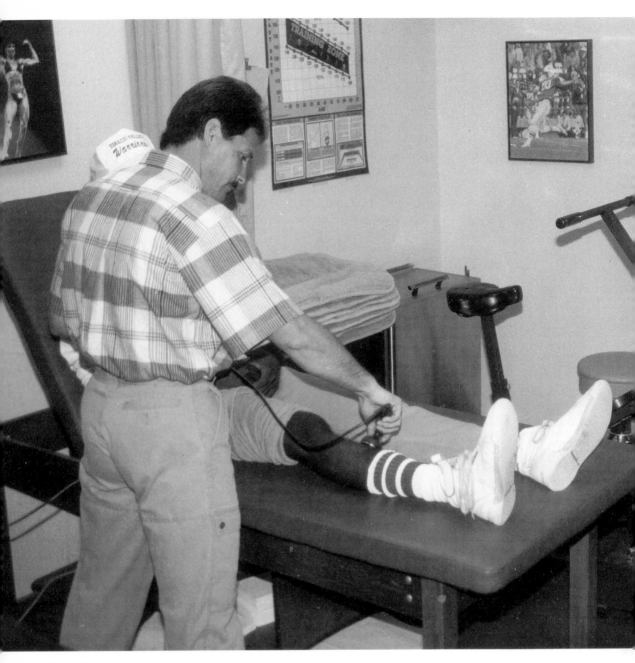

Developing techniques for pain control and improved movement after injury is a very important part of Dean Miller's work. He advises athletes, including riders, as to just what is possible after an injury.

than any sport in the world, I think. It sounds a little ridiculous, and maybe the triathletes and the marathon people are very conscious of their food and training, but racers are a little more scientific. Some of the triathletes may be overtraining in certain instances, whereas the racers are looking very carefully at what they need to do to succeed at their branch of the sport.

Europeans still have an advantage over Americans in that they can go home every week. Even if they don't go home they are more used to the environment. The Americans – Randy, Eddie, Freddie – all have to have expensive lifestyles, with big comfortable motorhomes, so they have an identifiable place there that is home. Their normal home is not just a hundred miles down the road. But things have got a lot more professional, to the point in Europe where the teams have their own cooks and can give the riders the food they need in the paddock. If Eddie wants pasta then the Marlboro chef will cook it for him; if Randy wants a special sort of food then his team can organise that.

Nutritionally if you are on the right diet you feel good all the time. If you rest well you will have more energy and that will make you better and smarter on the bike. But it's hard to see the difference that nutrition makes now, because everyone has pulled up their diet and fitness level. All the top guys are doing it, so the level has just advanced forward.

The thing I came up against, working with Randy when he rode for Kenny, is that Kenny would say, 'Randy can't have that food.' That may work for Kenny, but Randy is a very different sort of person. Diet is a very individual thing and when I design a diet I first ask, 'What kind of foods do you like?' Randy likes to eat steak occasionally, so let's put it in. It is better for him to be mentally satisfied but conscious of what he is doing, thinking, 'OK, I'll have the steak tonight but I know I can't have it tomorrow as well.' Or if the rider wants eggs and bacon for breakfast, fine, but not every day. I have to design a diet that will allow a certain flexibility but will taper down the unwanted foods. Kenny is a completely differently disciplined individual. He just says, 'OK, if I can't have the meat, I can't have the meat. I'll have the bread and cheese or whatever it takes.'

Everyone is different and you have to allow for that. You can't fight it. If you go to their motorhomes in Europe you can see that. Freddie decided he wanted a jacuzzi in his motorhome. Fine, he stays in a hotel, but likes a jacuzzi between practice sessions. If you go to their homes you can see the completely different way they live. Randy has a frantic existence. He has twenty-five cars to worry about, he'll be wondering where he is going to eat that night or what the latest business deal is. At Kenny's things are different. He is at home, he has kids and his bikes are there to ride when he wants and, to a certain extent, his business fits in around it. Eddie, he likes to be busy, he likes to train, go out riding and keep active. None of them are sit-down, calm sort of people, they are all self-motivated and know what they want. If we do go out to the restaurant and I order the food they are likely only to take three bites. If I gave them a diet and said, 'No meat', it would not be long before most of them would say, 'Hey look, I can't take this.'

Dirt tracking on the farm with the family and friends. Roberts leads the way on the XR100 Honda, ideal for developing skills without having to go so fast you risk getting hurt. Following his example are Kenny junior, Wayne Rainey and Bubba Shobert.

I try to be very individualistic and from the training point of view the same things apply, because everyone's style is very different. Kenny knew what he had to do. If I went to Kenny and said, 'I want you to do twelve of this specific exercise', then Kenny would do fifty because he knew that was right for him. That mental input is important. When he broke his back before the start of the '79 season no one thought he could race again yet he came back, raced, and won the World Championship. He had no problem because he knew how to push himself, how far he could go with the injury. Every champion I have ever met is a thinker. They have a high mental capacity or they don't get to the top.

Perhaps because Kenny had worked with himself for so long before I became involved, he was wiser than most. He had studied his own development and worked out what was best for him. That makes it tough now, as a team owner, because he wants to press the ideas that worked for him on to his riders and, as individuals, they resist.

In general terms we are trying to get racers to the point where 60-70 per cent of their diet is carbohydrate – pasta, high-grain cereal, fruit and vegetables. About 15-20 per cent should be fat which is butter, meat fat, milk, that type of food; then 10-15 per cent protein, which you are going to get from milk, meat and fish. That is the goal we shoot for and I have a computer with a dietary program, so I can sit down and design a diet for each individual, making some allowances for their likes and dislikes. It does not produce exact results, though, and you cannot always eat precisely what is on the diet. So, above all, you just have to be aware of what you are eating and what the dietary requirements are.

Along with that diet we push a lot of fluids, primarily water, and try to stay away from refined sugar. I don't want them drinking a whole lot of cokes, and I try and keep them off diet drinks just the same, because we don't know enough about the effect of the chemicals in them and what they do to the body. We don't really know what things like Nutrasweet and those kinds of additives do. Most of the research has been to see that they are not cancer-producing. OK, so they aren't, but they are a protein and we do not know enough about what they do in the body. So I would rather stick to water and the fruit juices, which are high carbohydrate and high energy stuff.

That kind of diet, with 60 per cent carbohydrate, is referred to as 'carbohydrate loading'. The old system used to be that you suppressed the carbohydrate level until you wanted the athlete to perform, then you loaded him up before the event and packed him with carbohydrate for energy. That is a good concept except that if you are training every day then you will be depleted in carbohydrates and never catch up when it comes to the race. The carbohydrate level needs to be higher all the time, so if I go out and exercise my athlete, and blow that carbohydrate out of his system, then he will be starving for more carbohydrate intake to replace what he has burned up.

The athletes I work with do not have too much of a problem with their diets, because their exercise programme tends to break down the body reserves early in the week. It depresses that carbohydrate

Dean Miller working with one of his athletes at his clinic in California. Training on equipment like this is only part of a programme and may be used to develop specific muscle groups.

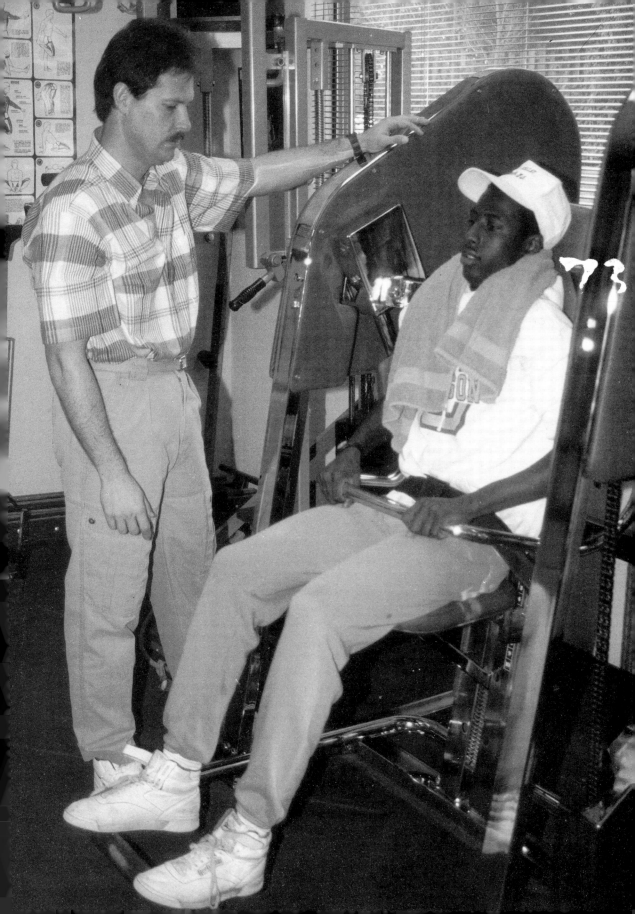
73

Those were the days, when the dividing line between a Grand Prix road race circuit and a motocross track was a fine one. Placing extra mental and physical demands on the rider, Imatra was dangerous more because of the telegraph poles than the railway lines but the level crossings took their toll on machinery and it is unlikely to be purely coincidental that Roberts suffered mechanical failures there. This was '79 though and Roberts recovered from a brush with the straw bales in the wet to finish sixth.

level, making the athlete desire pasta, fruit and vegetables. He carries on eating at a more or less constant level but the carbohydrate level goes up, because my training programme then includes a period of rest. My programmes are always based on a balance of work then rest. There has to be a direct relationship between stress and rest.

If a Grand Prix lasts, say, forty-five minutes, then that exertion is occurring normally on a Sunday. Everyone says they are training for race day, but they don't see it as part of a cycle. So, on a Sunday, whether they are racing or not, my riders should be able to go at 100 or 110 per cent both in physical stress and concentration. Then Monday is a rest day; they do nothing, so dropping from 100 per cent to zero. On Tuesday we go back to 95 or 100 per cent workload, as much as the body will take. Then Wednesday we drop off to about 60 per cent. If practice starts again for the Grand Prix on Thursday, and the riders are back on the track, we will drop down to about 20 or 30 per cent and they may just take a jog. If it is not a race week they may do 40-50 per cent workout. Friday and Saturday it's rest again, ready for maximum effort on Sunday.

If my riders are not racing on Sunday I still want them to work out hard. That blows the carbohydrate level out and then we build it up through the rest period on Monday, blow it out again on Tuesday, and allow it to build up again through Friday and Saturday, so there is plenty of energy available for race day on Sunday. The system is designed so that the energy capacity is higher on each successive Sunday, week to week, as the body is trained to make use of more energy. The level of carbohydrate intake, both as a percentage and an actual amount, remains the same but the body makes better use of it.

Most people are just trying to work flat out all the time, to achieve a peak of fitness and hold it. They work, work, work up to a point, but then drop off because they cannot hold that intense activity forever. With this system of balance, stress against rest, we work upwards with a series of plateaux.

Where we run into a few problems is that the Americans that road race fly back and forth to Europe. Airline flights are stressful, plus on a long-distance flight you can lose 20-30 per cent of the body fluid. They have to keep their fluid intake high, all the time on the flight, or when they get to the other end they would not be able to work out at 60 per cent.

Those workouts, which are hard twice a week, include a twenty- to thirty-minute road run, and a weight programme for strength and endurance in the muscles. Riding a bike comes into it as well, and Eddie might burn up a couple of tanks of gas in the day on his moto-crosser. That would be a tough workout. If you add up the half-hour run, the hour spent on the Nautilus, weight training and the hour and a half on a motocrosser, that is three hours' hard work. Do that twice a week.

That is only physical stress, though, and the mental side is also important. Racers lose weight in Europe just because of the pressure of worrying about World Championship points and so on. The more relaxed schedule on Thursday, Friday and Saturday is important as a balance against that. You cannot reproduce that mental stress situation in a training programme. The rider just has to learn to cope with it and you can see that they improve with experience.

The physical preparation, the exercises that the rider does, are not just for general heart-lung fitness but also for their ability to work the motor cycle. Racers use particular muscles. I have studied the way they ride the Grand Prix 500s and the muscles they use, and one thing that becomes obvious is that the way they are turning the bike at the end of the race is completely different from the beginning. They are using different muscles to work the bike and get it to do what they want it to do, because of the tyre wear. As the tyres begin to get more slippery the body position on the bike changes and the muscular pattern changes with it. In the last ten minutes of the race the rider is having to compensate for the machine, so he needs a strength factor late in the race.

Different riders have different requirements. If you watch Eddie he doesn't need a lot of strength, his style is very relaxed and stays that way. Randy, on the other hand, is almost too strong. He really works hard with the bike, forcing it around, and he runs into trouble at the end of the race when his strength level is down. McElnea is the same: he is a fast, skilled rider but works harder than Lawson, who tends to sit on the bike and let it do the work for him. With Randy we have to increase his muscular endurance rather than his strength.

Two different sorts of programmes are required, one for the racing season when the riders are in Europe most of the time, and the other for the winter when they are at home preparing for the next year. Before the season they need a programme that has variety and is building them up to a point where they are fit to start competition. During the season the programme still needs to have variety, to keep them interested, but it must be less stressful. The idea then is not to build strength but to keep it high while leaving energy for competition.

The last year I spent in Europe with Brad Lacky, doing the motocross World Championship, we made arrangements to use training equipment wherever we went. That meant that Brad was kept at a peak all season, and we could work properly between races. But the American road racers won't do that – they just want to fly home between GPs – and that concerns me. I am bothered that they lose water during the flights and it takes a lot out of them. It also leaves them little time at home to do anything, either to train or to get the stress rest which is just as important.

Road racing is very different from most other physical sports. You have to look closely at each sport really to understand what physical effort is involved. Take American football, for example, and the position of playing Defensive Back. He appears to play a strenuous sport, but realistically he is only in action for about six minutes per ball game. Yet he trains six hours a day for those short bursts of intense activity. Over the twenty games he plays a year that only adds up to 120 minutes of activity. That is two, or let's stretch it to three, hours of competitive activity per year. He has a special requirement because of the strength he needs to perform his job and the blows his body receives which generate an associated fatigue.

If you look at motocross, then it is total body involvement for two forty-minute motos in a Grand Prix. I don't think there is anything else as physical as that. If you fall down in a muddy race after thirty-five minutes, when your heart rate is up around 180, you have to be able to wrestle a bike upright that weighs well over two hundred kilos with the mud on it. That is strenuous. Motocross is just about the most strenuous sport, and if you train at that then you are going to find riding a road racer relatively easy, even though there are a few special requirements.

It is great to be able to work out at a gym, where you have all the best equipment and, hopefully, some good advice about what to do and what not to do. In most places it is possible to join a gym, but even if you can't there are things that anyone can do at home to improve their general fitness for racing. Push-ups, sit-ups, running, running in place, squats – anything which puts up the heart rate. If you run for twenty minutes and then do a series of exercises, push-ups, sit-ups, etc. slowly, while the heart rate is up, that is very fatiguing and that is good for your condition. Europeans do that a lot. Their idea is start stop, start stop, a variety of speed play and different activities that keep the heart rate up. Europeans have much better muscular endurance: they can take a ten-pound weight in their hand and work with it for an hour. The Americans, though, can take a one-

Roberts on the 500 at Oulton Park in 1983. One reason for his retirement was the stress on his body, particularly the forearm troubles which Roberts suffered in common with many other top riders.

hundred-pound ball and work with it fifteen or sixteen times while the Europeans could not do it once.

For road racing you need a combination of the two. You need strength to make the bike do what you want, all the way through, because getting that 500 to go where you want it to is taxing. But you also need that endurance, late in the race when the tyres have gone off.

When you are working out in the gym, and pushing your heart rate, you have to be aware that there are limits. Take your age away from 220 and that gives you the maximum safe heart rate (for the average person assuming there are no overriding medical problems). For a twenty-five-year-old the maximum rate is thus 195 beats per minute. Motocrossers do reach that point, road racers probably do not, although they may get to that level due to stress before the race. Once they settle into the race their heart rate is probably averaging between 140 and 170, or maybe 180. So, thinking that you might hit 180 at some point in the race, you want to train up to that. You must do some six minutes of warm-up before the training period, and then exercise at such a speed that your heart rate gets up to the desired level. Stop every ten minutes to count your pulse for six seconds and multiply by ten to measure how you are doing.

You have to consider that a road race Grand Prix is forty-five minutes long and that is what you have to train for, pushing your heart rate up to between 140 and 170 over that period, with perhaps an occasional peak at 180. You should then plot the achieved heart rate every time you exercise, to see how you are performing, and which area needs improving. Are you maintaining that stamina for the full forty-five minutes, and a little beyond, because there is no point in collapsing across the tank of the bike at the last corner. You have to think in terms of being race-fit for fifty minutes.

This pattern is not restricted to the gym. You should carry it over onto the track. At a test session, when you stop to change something on the bike, take your pulse and see how much effort you are actually using. That can give you an *idea* of what rate you require, but only if you are testing at race-winning speed and under something like racing conditions. And don't forget that the pressure of competition will also push your heart rate up.

The effort involved also varies from track to track. Some circuits allow a rest period on the straight, others hardly any at all, so it is no good practising at a track with a long straight and thinking that, because your heart rate is low, you do not need to push it. You can be sure that sooner or later you will find yourself racing for forty-five minutes on a track that will have your heart rate well up in the 170s.

Different circuits also affect different muscles as well: a place like Yugoslavia, with hard left-handers, is tough on that side of the body. Other circuits may have you changing direction all the time, or be particularly hard on the forearms because of heavy braking. You have to be prepared for this and push all your muscles so hard that they will last on any circuit. That's why training has to be harder than the actual thing.

At the end of your workout you should have a wind-down period. The heart rate should go down to where you started after the warm-up, to about 140. Then over the next five minutes it should come down 120, 115, 110, 100, 95, in steps of a minute.

What you are really trying to do is raise your level of aerobic exercise, i.e. exercise where the body is able to replenish the oxygen supply at the necessary rate to keep going. You can find out your aerobic rate by exercising up to the point where you can just keep going. The heart rate at that point is your maximum aerobic level. (It is, of course, lower than the maximum heart rate, which you only peak at.) Go past the aerobic point and you are at the anaerobic level where you cannot replace the oxygen that the muscles are using, and you will quickly be exhausted.

Of course, there are times through the racing career of any rider when he is going to get hurt. You have to be very careful with injuries, and get the very best medical advice, because abusing an injury is obviously going to lead to all sorts of long-term problems.

Decisions have to be made, like after Eddie Lawson's crash at

Laguna Seca in '86, in the middle of a season when he was trying to win his second world title. It was a bad crash, in which he could have died, but he was fortunate. He was left with a broken collarbone which had also popped out where it is connected to the sternum. It was necessary to look at his injury and the biomechanics of riding with it. How would it be affected by the movements demanded by racing the bike? I have the philosophy that it is better to be healthy for ten races than unhealthy for eleven. The points that you lose missing that one race in order to get fit can be made up against riding in all the races below par because you gave the injury no time to heal.

In Eddie's case I looked at the biomechanics and, because I understand the road racer and know what is going on when the rider is working the bike, I knew he would not have a problem with this particular injury. I have the equipment at my clinic to analyse injuries and work out what the effects are likely to be. So when the people I work with get hurt, I need to eliminate pain and increase their range of motion. I would never even consider working on an injured rider to get him competing again if that was going to cause him permanent damage.

When Eddie turned up at the next race, the French Grand Prix at Paul Ricard, I went with him to work against the pain and to make sure everything was as it should be. On the first day he was sore, and he did not go very fast. The second day was a little better, but he did not go flat out. Come Saturday, and the final session of practice, I insisted that he wear this bra that would hold his shoulders back. For two days he didn't want to wear it, but I knew he would feel better with it on. Just standing in his leathers it did not feel right, but on the bike, when he hit the brakes, it took the load off the injury and he didn't have any pain. He came in after a few laps and said it felt great. Then he went out and set the fastest time, a second quicker than anyone else.

For me there are no limits to what you can do, as long as it is safe. As long as it is not stupid we are going to go for it.

In all aspects of sports training, fitness and injury treatment you need the best advice and instruction for the best results. Search out an expert. In Europe they are called kinaesiotherapists. In America we call them physical therapists. The work has to go beyond merely looking after injuries: you need someone who can advise you on your whole fitness programme. Trainers may only look after the exercise programme, in which case you have to find a doctor or a therapist who can apply what we call modalities – the electrical stimulation, the ultrasound that are required to look after an injured athlete.

The problem with going to many doctors can be that they do not understand racing as a sport. They see kids at the hospital who have injured themselves on the road, or wherever, and they just see motor cycles as a bad deal. You have to try and explain what you do and how serious you are about getting fit and doing it properly: convince them to give you the sort of help you need.

There are some basic things you can do for yourself, to look after a bump, a bruise or a sprain – typical problems that everyone has from time to time. The main thing is to use ice, then you are way ahead of the game. Apply an icepack and elevate the injury so that the blood does not flood the area, twenty minutes on and twenty off, until the pain goes away. The thing is to get the blood to flow away from the injury. Without ice the blood will pack the area until it throbs with pain and you are immobilised. With a more serious injury the important thing is to get it looked at quickly, but ice can help here too, because it keeps the swelling down until you can get to the doctor or therapist. If it takes twenty-four hours before I see an injury, it will **,** take me another twenty-four hours to take care of the effects.

Chapter 12

Rivals

When I started riding I was attracted to the guys who were serious about their racing, Dick Mann, Mert Lawill, Cal Rayborn and Kel Carruthers. Those are the four people that I would have to say I was drawn to and admired the most. They also just happen to be the people who made it the furthest.

Dick Mann was a great racer who just went on and on. He was still racing professionally when he was almost forty years old, and in fact he still is racing. Lawill was good all the way through his career and he had the same sort of longevity as Mann. Rayborn was the road racer I probably admired most, but of course he was killed racing in New Zealand. Then there was Kel, who got all the way as a rider, helped me when I was starting racing and then went on to be my mechanic. It was the professionalism of these guys that impressed me more than their ability. Of course they had great ability too, but it was their professionalism that made the difference and that is what I admired.

They weren't my rivals. By the time I came into the arena they were past their peak, although Kel was still riding well. I was the young rider of the new era and my main competitor at that time was Gary Scott. We weren't just competing on road racers but on the dirt as well, and he was racing Harleys. He was good on the dirt, on the miles, but not so hot on the road, so I didn't have any rivals that I could really compare with on ability until I came to Europe.

My first rival was Agostini. I raced him at Daytona and then we went on to Imola. The thing that impressed me about Ago was that he was a very determined rider. He had to have everything working just right and then he would really ride the motor cycle. I know he spent a lot of time working on the bike to make it better – if it wobbled he didn't like it – and I spent a lot of time analysing the guy. It seemed to me that he pushed the bike to the limit, made it work to that limit where he was really pushing the front end. He was pushing the front end harder than I was because that was how he wanted it to steer, using the front wheel where I was using the back. I didn't learn anything from it, though, because I had already seen Kel do it and he had been my teacher rather than a rival.

I was faster at that time when I first raced Ago, even though I hadn't had much road racing experience, because I could ride the 700. I think that Ago was probably better on the 500s than he was on the 750s because of his style. I didn't actually learn anything from Ago while we were racing nose to tail. It is hard to learn anything from another guy while you are riding with him. I learnt that he was a front end rider and that he went into corners faster than I did but I came out faster. We were just two different

types of riders. I considered Ago a very, very good rider but I don't think that the 750 was his cup of tea. Of course, Kel would point out that the guy used different lines from me, and that he was used to dangerous circuits. I didn't know anything about that sort of thing. I knew what I wanted to do: I was just trying to put it all together before I killed myself.

When we went to Imola he knew the circuit but, because I was happier than him on the 750, we were going faster and beating him pretty bad. When I pulled in for gas I had about a thirteen-second lead on him. I was a long time in the pits and Ago got into the lead. He stopped later and his stop was quicker. I was riding around, not going too fast, and he came out onto the track in the lead. I didn't realise the position until I saw him in front with a few laps to go. Kel thought I knew that he was in front but I didn't. Ago was pretty smart. He knew he wasn't going to beat me flat out in that race so he used his brain and that was something I wasn't used to. He had a lot more experience than me and he used it: he just rode round and we made the mistakes. That is why I needed Kel so much at first, to tell me what was going on.

It was the 750 that put me ahead of the other American riders from the start, guys like Gene Romero who had been riding the 750 Triumphs and BSAs. At the first tyre tests we did at Daytona on the 700 Yamahas I remember doing 2m 12s while they were doing 2m 17s. I adapted to it real quick.

After Ago the next guy I considered a rival was Barry Sheene. I first came up against him at the Easter Match Races in England but, because the 750 Suzuki was not that competitive, I didn't really think of him as a rival until I met him on a 500 at the Grands Prix. Everyone considered that the Yamaha was better than the Suzuki and no one took the Match Races 100 per cent seriously, especially the British guys. To them it was just another meeting, though to the Americans it was a bit more than that. We wanted to prove that we were as good as anyone.

It was not until I came to Europe to do the Grands Prix, the year after Baker came over, that Sheene started to become a rival. He was the World Champion and obviously he was the guy I was going to have to beat.

Stevie was awful fast for one year, '76. He flat beat me at Laguna. We were having a real bad year dirt track wise and we were not very up when it came time for Laguna. He was ready for Laguna and I wasn't. It was as simple as that. Stevie beat me and then went to Europe right after Laguna for the '77 season.

Stevie was a real front end rider and, like all front end riders, he depended on it too much. These guys start to fall down, get leery of the front end and then they can't go fast. It is like a pro golfer who is leery of putting too fast – but if you don't putt past the hole the ball will never go in. It is the same with racing. You have got to be able to go past the limit or you won't be the fastest. But if you go past the limit with the front end you crash. With the back you have a chance to save it and it is much easier to get your confidence up. If you are a front end rider you have to be on such a narrow edge to go fast, and keeping the bike on two wheels is hard. If you start falling off you lose that edge and then you have lost the whole game. That's what happened to Stevie, and he is not the only one. A rear end steering rider doesn't lose it as often, so he keeps his confidence up.

It's also easier to learn race tracks if you ride from the rear, because you only have to get on the gas when you know where you are going. You don't have to go into the corner over your head and not knowing where you are going. That is why it was a lot harder for Stevie to learn the GP circuits in his first year than it was for me.

Sheene was a big rival, then, and so was Hansford. But I got on so well with Gregg that I couldn't really call him a rival. When you like a guy like that it can be difficult, and he was real likable, though I never had to get angry with people to beat them. We raced a lot, especially in the 250 class. He beat me and I beat him. I enjoyed racing with Gregg. I thought he had a lot of natural talent, probably the most natural talent for just getting on the bike and riding it.

Kork had talent, too. I didn't consider that he had as much natural talent as Gregg but he was building on it all the time, going faster and faster. When I raced against him he was just at the beginning, in the early stages, where he had not yet got the confidence to dominate the 250 class like he did later. Korky rode what I considered was more of a neutral style, a balance between the front and back. Gregg rode more on the front end. Korky didn't ride completely with the rear end but more than the Europeans did. Gregg was a heavy braker and heavy on the front end.

When you race against a good friend like Gregg it does affect the way you do things. I guess I wouldn't try the same sort of passing manoeuvres that I might with someone else. It doesn't make a lot of difference but I would not elbow my way past Gregg, I wouldn't go 110 per cent to beat him but I would go that far to beat Sheene. Sheene annoyed me because he whined so much to the press. If I won Gregg would say, 'So you beat me, you...', but Sheene would whine about his tyres or something. It was interesting to see what he was going to whine about next.

Sheene was a friendly sort of guy, though, always free with the advice. When I first went to a Grand Prix in '74 with the 250 he was there to tell me how to push-start the bike. He told me I needed to use the choke, Kel was saying I didn't, but between the two I guess I got it started pretty good. Then at my first Grand Prix on the 500 in Venezuela he was giving me advice about how screwed up the Yamaha was, how the bike was too small. He wanted me to sit on his Suzuki and see that it was a bigger bike and felt more comfortable. I didn't want to sit on the thing. I thought my Yamaha was real comfortable. I didn't know too much about GP racing but I thought it was fine. He was showing me his shocks with no springs; I felt there was no way that would work, from what I knew about dirt track, and after that race they got thrown down the road.

He was a nice guy and wanted to help people, which was OK until they turned into the main competition. Looking back on it now, I think that Sheene had to get his rivals going to make himself go faster. I can't think of any other reason for it. Sheene needed someone to race against. He knew that one man winning everything didn't make a story for the press and he was one of the best talkers with the press I have ever seen. He would say all sorts of things to the press about me but I just used to laugh at him. It never got me mad to the point where I did something silly, but it did make me push a lot harder than I would to beat someone like Hansford. That sort of psychological game never worked with me. I saw

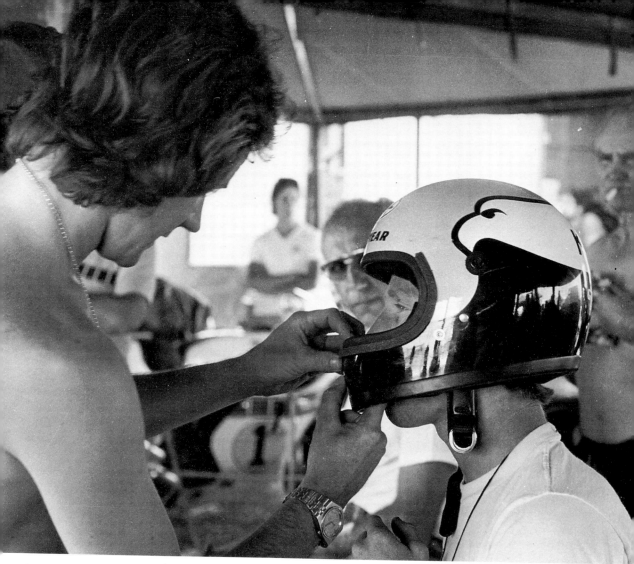

Sheene was very helpful to Roberts early in 1978, his first full Grand Prix season. Here the reigning champion gives some advice about a helmet vent during practice for the Venezuelan Grand Prix that kicked off the season.

through it. You have to. I think Sheene was a nice guy who didn't want everyone to see that he was a nice guy.

I enjoyed beating him a lot. The most important thing was beating him the first year, because no one had ever come and won the 500 title like that. It was also Goodyear's first time in Europe, and Yamaha didn't know if I could ride their bike or not. American Yamaha knew I could do it but Japan didn't: they thought Baker had beaten Kenny and Baker couldn't beat Sheene. All that, added to the fact that Sheene said I couldn't do it and that I wouldn't be a threat, made him the biggest rival even before the season started.

The main thing about Sheene was he was good and safe to ride with. I enjoyed racing him and we had some great races. He had ability. I think that if he had spent more time working on his riding and less time working on his mouth then he'd probably have been even tougher to beat than he was – but I am glad he didn't. Despite all the advice I don't think that I learnt from him. What I learnt I learnt by myself, with Kel's help. I was the first guy to start dragging my knees, and steering with the rear wheel, and that separated me from the others. Sheene and I were as different as night and day: he rode with the front and I rode with the rear.

There was no one else at that time that I thought was as good as Sheene. Ferrari ended up second one year but I never rated him that highly and he never got it together again after he crashed at Le Mans. He was not that consistent. At some races he would impress me, then other races he wasn't quite there, he would just be a tad off, accelerating a bit late, braking a little early.

Next along were Randy and Lucchinelli. Lucchinelli was the most flamboyant guy of anyone I ever raced against. Sometimes I'd follow him and he would go into the corner so deep and so fast, just throwing it in, that I would think: 'Wow!! He has just got to crash.' But that year, '81, he just kept getting away with it. He was extremely crazy. When you are riding against someone like that you have to give them a lot of room, and you have to plan on beating them over the whole season, not in one race. That was a good year for him: he had a good team, a good bike and he rode well.

Uncini was completely different. He came out of the woodwork in '82 and really shocked me. He jumped into Luccinelli's team and just split. He made everybody look silly. Then again, it was all on the front end. I have never seen anyone brake so hard and flick the motor cycle in as Franco did at some races. It freaked Randy right out because he was on the Suzuki as well and everyone thought he was the threat to take the title. Randy and I were on Dunlops that year and they just didn't work like the Michelins. Franco used to come and say to me that he couldn't slide the front; he couldn't believe how good it was and he was ready to make use of it. He was not like Lucchinelli. Uncini was a quiet thinker, a very intelligent person, and he thought about his racing. He had the right tyres on the right bike and he made use of them.

Randy was never a real threat to me. Things would happen to him when it looked as though he might win the World Championship – he would have a bad race or have a fork seal pop out. It just seemed that every time the pressure was on, to win a race, to win the World Championship, something would happen. I never really considered him a threat. If everything was equal he was a good rider, but never dominant.

Freddie was the first dominant rider that I'd raced since I hit Europe. When he arrived in '82, he just wanted to win worse than anything else and he had the natural talent to back it up. Even Sheene at his best would have been no threat to Freddie. Sheene was harder to figure, like Uncini: you never knew when they were going to go fast, but with Freddie I knew he always wanted to go fast every time he got on the motor cycle.

Since I stopped racing it has been between Gardner and Lawson. Gardner has the ruthless, 'I want to win no matter what' attitude and he rides the motor cycle real good. Eddie is more of the quiet, 'I'll get even' sort of guy, who just goes faster and faster. I was worried about Eddie taking over my spot at Yamaha at the end of '83 because I felt that he had not progressed much that year. But in Eddie's own quiet little way he'd progressed quite a lot, he just wasn't willing to show it at that time, and he kept on getting better slowly.

As far as longevity is concerned, and thinking about someone who is going to be at the top year after year, then you have got to look at Eddie. He has his own inner fire smouldering away. It is something personal. Ago can be messing around, doing whatever, and Eddie takes no notice. Eddie

Cal Rayborn as British fans remember him. He came to the Match Races in 1971 and shook the locals by sharing the wins with Ray Pickerel, although when this picture was taken in 1972, he was not so dominant. He had already won Daytona twice, in '68 and '69, but that meant little across the Atlantic. It was the first time that Britain had seen what the Americans could do and they had not even heard of Kenny Roberts.

Kork Ballington. One of the greats according to Roberts, he won his first Grand Prix at Barcelona in Spain in 1976 on his private 350 Yamaha. Still a privateer, he scored a 250/350 double at Silverstone in 1977 and was signed to ride the factory Kawasakis in 1978. He won the 250 and 350 Championship double for them that year and again in 1979 but Kawasaki were never able to give him a competitive 500.

174

Roberts chasing Lucchinelli at Spa when the two were battling for the 1981 World Championship. Roberts led but the Italian steadily overhauled him. With three laps to go it was anyone's race and the two swapped places at every other turn. Arriving at the hairpin for the last time, they had to lap Michel Frutschi. Roberts went outside and Lucchinelli inside, the Italian stealing the advantage. The photograph shows how little there was in it coming out of the corner and heading for the finish line, but it cost Roberts three points.

is just Eddie and Eddie is going to win because Eddie wants to and not because anybody else wants him to. That's different from a lot of other guys – and Eddie is a very different person to work with.

These riders are from a different era and I can't really compare them with myself. Of those I raced against Freddie Spencer was definitely the number one rider. He was the most ruthless and had the most talent, which were perfectly matched together at that time, '83. If you are talking about pure talent I would have to say that Hansford came close to Freddie, but he just lacked the desire to smoke everybody. Gregg just had fun doing what he did and he had the talent to do it. I think he had more fun in the pits than Freddie ever did racing. Overall you have to put Freddie first when it comes to winning races. I'd put Gregg number two, just ahead of Korky, with Eddie fourth because he was still learning the year I rode with him. I've never raced against Gardner, except in the Suzuka Eight Hour, and that's not the same as riding a 500. I would say that Eddie and Wayne have the talent of Gregg Hansford. If you put all four of them together on the day, all riding at their best – Freddie, Eddie, Wayne and Gregg – they might finish in that order on determination, but it would be real close. Then there are people like Kevin Magee and Wayne Rainey. They've got a great deal of talent and will show a few people what they can do.

One thing that Freddie did, that none of the others have quite done, is go so fast off the start. I could do it but I thought it was pretty foolish. Usually when I got into second place Freddie would have eight seconds on me but I could still beat him. I never led a Grand Prix on the first lap. Any time you have a six-second lead it can be a psychological advantage, but you have to be able to make use of it, by holding it. If you are behind you have to have the confidence in your own ability to start knocking those seconds off. It is very disturbing to a rider like Freddie to see his pit board saying '+8', then '+7' and '+6'. He would know it was all over when you were knocking half seconds off his time every lap and he was going as fast as he could. In a Grand Prix, if I was catching Freddie at half a second a lap and the gap got down to three seconds, he would pull over and let me by. That is how psychologically damaging it is. Then he would follow. It is a lot easier to follow, but it is something else to set about knocking half a second a lap off someone who has an eight-second lead on you after just three laps. That is where the real determination and concentration comes in, eating away a few tenths at a time.

You must have that determination every time you go to the line. You have to know that you are going to give everything. I always went to the line thinking I was going to win. Randy seems to go to the line thinking, well, if it all goes well I can get second or third. I never did that. It is not in my mentality. Even on a bike that isn't good enough there are riders who go to the line every time thinking they are going to win. That is Mike Baldwin's attitude, no one out there is better than him.

You don't have to go to the line with a blind faith in your ability to win every race, because sometimes the circumstances might dictate that you cannot win because of the bike, or the tyres, or your experience. The most important thing is to go to the line knowing that you are going to *give* 100 per cent. There were times when I would get second or third

place and I knew that no one else in the world could have done that on that particular motor cycle. There were times when I got fifth that I knew no one else could have *rode* that motor cycle. I remember riding the OW61 and scaring everyone because it was trying to throw me off. I just wanted to do my job on my particular motor cycle better than anyone else. That is winning in itself and that is what I try to get through to the guys in my team. I want them to ask themselves where they are at in their ability with respect to riding that motor cycle 100 per cent.

It took me years to achieve what I considered was 100 per cent in terms of concentration, muscle tone, endurance, riding techniques and everything. Every year I got better and every year I worked on it. Who cares who wins or loses? The important thing is how we are riding the motor cycle. That is what I try to get through to my guys. If they are riding at 80 per cent and come second I am bummed out about it. If they ride at 100 per cent to get fifth I am happy. It took Randy a while to understand that. He had to programme himself in practice to run at 100 per cent but I think that in '87 you saw a different Randy Mamola than you have ever seen before, because he was riding in practice to push himself. We had some mishaps, like not having the concentration up, running off the race track, braking too hard, things which he still needed to work on after he stopped riding for our team.

Kevin and Wayne are different. They're so keen that they'll go on, lap after lap, testing in the freezing cold with not one complaint. They won't stop. There is no 'When is my flight out? Where is my Mercedes?' It is a whole different world working with those two. When they come in they are self-critical: they say they are not doing this right, or that, and we discuss it, work it out and make progress. I think that a lot of riders, especially Europeans, look at winning races when what they should be looking at is how to get better and push themselves to 110 per cent. You have to work at that and figure out where you are with respect to the rest of the riders. If you are riding at 110 per cent and Wayne Gardner smokes you, then you obviously don't have the talent. But if Wayne Gardner smokes you and you are only riding at 80 per cent then you have something to work on. That is how Eddie works, pushing his talent a little more every year, getting better all the time. Freddie didn't do that. His attitude to racing is different. He just sat back and said, 'Hey, I've got the best bikes, I'm wonderful, I'm faster than everybody else.' And it didn't work because the other guys kept clawing away and working on themselves to go faster. That is what happens to every great guy in the end: someone comes along that wants it more than he does.

Chapter 13

Team manager

Actually it is different for everybody, and everyone has their own idea on how to run a team. My team manager role is a little different from many others. The first thing is that I do not feel that I would make a good team manager in the usual sense of the word, because I don't have the time to do all the many, many things required every day. A team manager has to do a great deal of work, day in and day out, follow up to make sure that everything that is supposed to happen does happen. That is why I have someone else to do that and I concentrate on the overall direction of the team and working closely with the riders.

The day-to-day work is done by Paul Butler. His job is the groundwork and making sure that people do what they are supposed to do and what they promised to do. If I have a meeting with Dunlop and we agree to go testing in Malaysia then it is up to Paul to book the hotels, the flights, to make sure that the personnel are there, that the track is available and the machinery will be ready for the tests.

The only management that I do is to work with sponsors, to sort out the deals for the team, and I also concern myself with the overall image of the team. I make sure that the team is made up of the right people and produces what the sponsor requires both in terms of results and public image. At the end of the day I am responsible for everything because I am the team owner and if the team is not successful then it is to me that everyone eventually looks, not anyone else. The sponsors may decide that they would like to do a particular race or series but they look to me to tell them whether or not it is a good idea from the team's point of view. If I don't get the right results, or the right amount of press coverage, then it comes back to me eventually.

My strong point is, of course, being able to assist the riders in various ways so that they might be able to do a little bit better. I might not want the riders to do some particular PR work, because they'd have to be at the track four days before practice to do it, then perhaps another week for the race, and then travel from there to the next race – so it would all be too much and could affect their performance. Or I might advise what hotel they stay at or whether they might stay at the track.

When it comes to deciding when we should go testing there are probably four key people that contribute to the decision and they are Dunlop, because they make the tyres; Yamaha, because they may have things on the bike that need testing; Paul Butler; and myself. I may want to go testing because of tyres, the bike, or whatever, but it is Paul who has to get it organised and make it happen. So four different people have a say in the testing. It all has to be decided to try and make the riders perform at their best. These are all things that I have to do.

When I first came to Europe Kel Carruthers was the team manager. He is still a team manager but he is technical manager, which is what I am really. He works with the bikes and the riders, but of course I am closer to the riders and he has more to do with the bikes.

It is very important to get the right people in the team and that can be more important than having people who are the best of friends with each other. There are different ways of getting on with each other and the problem with motor cycle racing is that it is a very competitive sport and depends very much on the individual. Even the mechanics, though they are a different sort of people from the riders, are still competitive. They do all their work to make their rider on their bike go faster. They are competitive enough to want their rider to win, because that obviously reflects on them. More important, though, is that all the mechanics in the team work together and they do a great job, that is what makes them thoroughbreds. The riders are the only ones who, at the end of the day, are single individuals.

All the people in the team are, you hope, the best of their kind. You are trying to control a team of thoroughbred horses, not a pack of carthorses. They have personalities that are different from the average people.

Like most teams we have two riders and it is very difficult to get these individualists to work as one team. Each rider wants to beat the other and they are likely to run over each other to do it. You cannot stop that, so you have to find a way to work around it all the time. If you could get the two to stop fighting you would end up with a less competitive team, or at least with a number one rider and a number two, and then the number two would be less competitive. You don't get that too much in Grand Prix racing because the riders are all good and very competitive.

Mike Sinclair is in charge of what goes on with the motor cycles. I give some input. We do not always agree what should be done, but things get worked out. One difference is that he is very conscious of the time-frame he is working in and what can be done in that period. I am not so aware of that, so I sometimes suggest things that cannot be done in the time available. I am in between the riders and the engineer. I want to try and get things done to the bikes that will help the riders go faster.

You can easily get into the situation of trying to change too much and confuse the situation. There is only so much time available at the Grands Prix and very often what the rider needs is just to ride the bike and try to get down to the lap time he should be doing.

That is the thing about having a team manager with some experience. He should be able to help. There was one time in '86 that I was watching Mike Baldwin in practice at Monza, and I could see he was having problems coming through the last chicane onto the back straight – it was important because the speed down there can make a lot of difference. It was obvious that the bike was geared wrong and was making revs too

Kenny Roberts Team Manager passes the time with Rob McElnea and Tadahiko Taira.

early in the corner and sliding around too much if he got on the gas. He needed to have it bogging through the middle of the turn so that it was on the pipe as he hit the kerb coming out of the turn. After practice I told him that it would not work in the race. He trusted me enough to change the gearbox, even though there was no practice left, only the race-day warm-up session. It is certainly not something that you should usually do, go out to race anything you have not tried. But after the race he said he had gone faster and that the other gearbox would never have worked.

The riders need someone like Kel, Mike or me, a team co-ordinator or chief mechanic who understands them. I know I did. It's too much to be out there on your own and just have people pat you on the back when you come into the pits, telling you how well you are going. You are out there trying to test tyres, trying to test suspension and find out when either of them might go off, trying to work out whether the suspension has enough bump damping, rebound damping in three different areas, how the front forks are working, too soft, too hard. Thinking about all these things plus watching out for the other riders – frankly you can do with some help at times.

I try to be as careful as I can with the way I speak to the riders, but there are only so many ways you can say that they are not doing it right. It is best to avoid saying that, and ask if there is any way that you can help, ask about any problems with the bike. It is no good telling the rider he is too slow, because going fast has a lot to do with confidence. The rider must have confidence in himself and the machine. He also has to feel that everyone is behind him. I know that I needed to feel that everyone was 100 per cent behind me, or I could not give it 100 per cent effort. I always knew that Kel was right behind me, even though very often I did not get along with him. We often disagreed about many things, about how the bike should be set up, what tyres to run, and so on. I still knew that when we got out on the track he was 100 per cent behind me.

You don't have to be personal buddies, though of course it makes things more pleasant. The thing about Kel was that he was always think-ing for me as much as possible. If it looked like rain he would just pop his head inside the motorhome and say, 'What tyre do you want if it rains?' and I'd say, 'The A35', and he would say, 'That's what I thought' and he'd be gone. You need that type of backup, or at least I did.

It is not easy to be a team manager and stand there watching the riders instead of doing it yourself. It would be a lot easier if I never made sugges-tions and just watched without interfering. Once you have suggested something, though, you become responsible. If you never made any suggestions then you could always stand there and say, 'Well, you messed that up' – but once you have made that input they can turn round and say the same to you. The bottom line is that we have to make the riders go fas-ter. It does not matter who makes the decision, but someone has to. If you are not prepared to then you should get out the way, because the riders have to get on with going fast.

I have to choose riders that will not only give 100 per cent but will also work with the press, the sponsors and the public. That is part of their game, like it or not. No one is going to get paid to lock themselves up in the motorhome. In my career I always thought it was odd that the English

One of the team manager's jobs is to take some of the pressure off the riders. He has to know how to handle the press and get value for his sponsors while preserving a good working environment for the team.

184

journalists would say, 'Well, we can't talk to Roberts' when I cannot remember ever refusing to speak to someone. I remember reading all the bad quotes in the magazines the next week, but the only contingent of people that would not come to the motorhome after the race and get my views on what had happened were the English. The Italians, French, Dutch, Spaniards and the rest would always come by. I stayed at the track in the motorhome and that motorhome was virtually the team base until Ago came along with his bus. I didn't buzz off to the hotel, so I was always available and I think that is important because it is part of your job. It can be frustrating, though, because you can only be available, you cannot force anyone to listen or to print what you say.

I encourage riders to take the time to talk to the press. If the journalist then gets the story wrong, then they get it wrong and there is nothing you can do about it. But if you don't speak to them at all then they will always get it wrong. They will never get it right unless they can talk to you. Of course, riders are all highly strung individuals and they take pressure different ways. Some read the articles written about them in magazines and get upset.

I occasionally got upset about things that were written about me, and twice I phoned magazines. Once it was because they were on about start money, and whether or not I should receive what I was getting. I didn't feel it was anyone else's business how much money I received, it was between me and the promoter: he paid the amount he thought I was worth and the press had no business saying he shouldn't. You can ask whether or not Elton John is worth half million dollars a show, but who can say? If the people want to pay to see him, then he is. This magazine was comparing me to the average factory worker. The other thing that made me ring up was the press attitude to the World Series. We were trying to get something organised and they just seemed to do anything they could against it. One thing they printed on the front page was that Kork Ballington had signed with Kawasaki to do the World Championship: 'First rider to leave World Series.' Kork was furious because he had not said that and had not signed any contract. I met both English papers and they printed a rebuttal, but it was about an inch high on page seven. I hardly felt that was fair or truthful.

I don't care what is printed as long as it is truthful. If I am an idiot then say so. But if you are going to be successful you have to accept that things are going to be written about you that you don't like. You just have to accept that. You have to put up with the fact that even if they listen to what you say, they will only use pieces of it, and it will not come out sounding like you meant it to sound. It will do you no good to ring up and complain, or to sound off at the journalist. All you can do is be available and be honest and hope that they listen and print an honest story.

There are things that you should not talk about, of course. You are employed by a sponsor or a factory, and you know that there are things that are secret or that they do not want the press to know about. Sometimes you have to be very careful what you say. I try to be honest with everyone, but with technical secrets it is difficult. You have to say that you don't know, or better still, just point out that you cannot say what is going on with the bike or next year's machine.

When it comes to giving opinions about things, you should also watch what you say. Do not get into criticising other riders, it will only end up looking bad. Back in the '70s I could easily have got into a mudslinging match in the press with Barry Sheene, but that was not my strategy. When Sheene started the rock-throwing he wanted me to come back at him, but I knew the chances were that what I said would not come out right in the press, so I said nothing. My honest opinion was that Sheene was a very good rider. His opinion was that I wasn't a very good rider and if he had my tyres, my bike, Kel Carruthers and so on he would be winning. My feeling was that I didn't want to give Sheene or the press any ammunition, and that if I beat him then I beat a very good rider. That was the way I played it, but he kept digging himself further and further into the hole.

You can use the press to your advantage, too, and I did at one time or another. When I refused to reply to Sheene and tell him that he was a stupid idiot, like they expected, that was using the press. I had people, members of the public, come up to me at the end of that season and tell me they thought Sheene was making an ass out of himself in the papers, and they were glad that I was not getting into that. There were English people apologising for the way he was acting and I could see no sense in what he was doing. It wasn't winning him any points and I was in the business long term so I wasn't interested in a short-term battle of words.

It is a lot more difficult to be truthful as a team manager because it may look very bad on one of my riders if they make the wrong decision about, say, tyres. I am not going to go to the press and say what an idiot he was and he made the wrong choice. Admitting he made a mistake is up to the rider, and I like to think that I admitted my mistakes, like when I ran off the track at Monza in '83. Ago was telling the Italian press that there was a brake problem, but I pointed out to them what they wanted to know, that I had screwed up and misjudged my speed passing a tail-ender. They expected me to make an excuse and could hardly believe that I was just saying, 'Hey look, I'm human, I screwed up.'

Loyalty to the team and to the factory is also important. There is no point in spending all your time cursing the bike or the team, you have to make the best of the situation. I stayed with Yamaha all through my racing career and they appreciated that. I stuck with their development projects even when it did not seem to be helping me win races. When the V four was causing so much trouble there were several times when they asked me if I wanted to ride the OW60, until they got the OW61 sorted out, but I said, 'No, I don't want to ride the OW60, I'm in it with you guys and we'll get this one sorted out. If we go down then we are all going down together.'

There were times when I talked about leaving Yamaha and riding for someone else. But even after the OW61, which was so bad, I never seriously thought about going because I knew the engineers, knew the motor cycle and knew we could get things worked out. That was not so much down to loyalty as the fact that I knew what we had to do to get a motor cycle that worked and I was confident that the Japanese engineers could do it.

As a professional rider you are paid to present the right image to the public and the press, but you should certainly speak your mind behind closed doors. I did many times. I got so mad in one meeting at Yamaha

Choosing riders for a team can be very difficult. Roberts appreciates the attitude of the Australians Wayne Gardner and Kevin Magee.

that I climbed across the table to get at one engineer who had started laughing at what I was saying about the bike we needed for the coming season.

When I was racing dirt track in America I would line up on the Yamaha with fourteen Harleys. I had no chance on earth of winning the race, but I rode the wheels off that bike because I have always had the attitude that Yamaha were my company and I work for them. The result is that I still have a contract with the Yamaha Motor Corporation after seventeen years of racing and my pay cheque has never gone down. I think that a rider has to have that sort of commitment. He is either for the team or against it, and what is he going to gain by being against it? If you demand 100 per cent from your mechanics you must give the same.

I think that the damage that Freddie Spencer did himself, with his lack of commitment in '86, would take three or four seasons to make up, if it ever could be put right. My only complaint about Freddie is that he has never been honest with the press. According to him he has never lost a race, there has always been a tyre problem or a bike problem.

When it comes to choosing riders for a team I think that what is most important is the determination to win. For example, Wayne Gardner has it. To him winning is a business and that is what he wants to do. Unlike many Europeans and some Americans, he does not have a hang-up about being a star. Being a hero is not a big thing with him. He wants to get on with winning motor cycle races and make the money he should make in that position.

As far as young riders are concerned, I look for the same thing – that desire and determination to succeed in a very demanding, high pressure sport. I cannot afford to put my name behind someone who does not have the drive and perseverance to make it through. A major part of what makes a champion is determination, it's more important than natural talent, because there is so much that you can learn and work at.

It is determination that always drives you to be better. I guess that I had a certain amount of natural ability to ride a motor cycle. I went to Europe with less than twenty road races under my belt and put it over on Ago pretty bad at Imola, which was home for him. That did not mean that I was a great road racer. I still had a lot to learn and I was determined to improve. I went back to Europe to race the 500 in '78 and won the Championship. I won again in '79 and '80, but my riding was changing all the time. My drive was pushing my ability forward all the time.

In '81 I sized up Freddie when I raced against him a few times. I realised that he was good and I felt that one of the drawbacks of the way I was racing was that I didn't use the front tyre enough. I was slowing down a little bit more than I needed to, going into the corner. Probably there was 1 or 2 per cent of the front tyre I was not using and leaving as a safety margin. I felt that Freddie was relying strictly on the front tyre – a lot of the time he was pushing the front harder than I did – and since I saw him as the next threat I had to change my style a little bit and use more of the front tyre if I was going to beat him. So during the off-season that is what I worked on, thinking about it and how I was going to do it. Of course, it takes a little more concentration so I was working on that at the same time, with the food that I ate and the exercises I was doing to help me keep my concentration up all the way through the race.

I came out in 1982 to be one of the hardest guys on front tyres and stayed that way. I was pushing my ability all the time. I suppose that everyone needs some sort of natural talent, and there are all sorts of factors that come into riding success that we have no control over, but the most important thing is still the determination to push your ability and make the best of it. There are plenty of guys who obviously have a lot of natural ability but never make it, so determination has to be the biggest thing.

In my opinion I had twice as much natural ability as Gary Scott, but when we were riding dirt track in the States Scott was one of my biggest rivals. He would try so damned hard all the time and never give up. He would be battling for fourth place, trying harder than the guys around him. I'd be out in the lead and then my bike would break. Then second would break, then third and Scott would win, but he would never have

been there at all had he not been so dogged and determined. We would get to a TT that you could ride and I'd make him look silly. We would then go to a slippery old notched half-mile and he would make me look silly. I would be out there, sliding all over the place, trying to go faster than everybody else, and he would just be inside, following the pole, which in my view was being a pussy. Hell, I wanted to go faster than everyone else, but there were times when I had to realise that I couldn't.

The thing about motor cycle racing is that there are not enough trainers around to look after the riders. We need more people who know about diets and exercise. There are too few trainers, and also too few riders who realise that they need them. I have worked with Dean Miller since '79 and he has helped Randy and Eddie, working out training programmes and helping with injuries. He travelled to France with Eddie, after he hurt himself in the crash at Laguna Seca in '86, and I don't think that Eddie could have raced at the French GP if it had not been for Miller.

Most guys do their own thing and they just don't know enough. Many riders would do better if they had a trainer, because if they were fitter they could be racing harder at the end of the race. I can help riders with advice on riding and give them some ideas on what they should be trying out on the track, but their own bodies will be the limiting factor a lot of the time. I stay at home mostly, so I am not looking over my riders' shoulders asking them what they have been eating or how they have been training. Each rider needs someone to look after that sort of thing if they want to be the best. If I didn't win the World Championship each year, I wanted to know why. Most of the time when I finished down the ratings I knew why, either the equipment was way off par or it broke down. If I had the remotest idea that it was me that was lacking then I said to myself, 'Well, what is wrong, how can I be better?' That is all I thought about in the winter, how I could improve, and then I would work at it. That is what finally burnt me out of racing. It had been my attitude right from day one and in the end I had had enough of the training and the pushing myself physically all the time.

Fans, autographs are something else. I am not big on autographs, I would rather shake someone's hand and say 'Nice to see you'. It is very time-consuming and can get out of hand at a race meeting, so I never tell my riders to go and sign autographs. In the paddock we are working and should be left to get on with it. Of course, there is a time and place for everything, and shows are the place to sign autographs. I was never keen on being put in the situation of signing autographs, though.

I have never been my own mechanic as such, but I did work on racing motors when I was a junior with Yamaha. That made me feel better about the motor cycle, because I wanted to know what was going on with the machine. At first, when I rode for the factory, Yamaha were very, very reluctant to tell me what was going on with the machines or show me things. They never showed riders things so when I asked to see a cylinder they couldn't understand why. If I had not worked hard at understanding the machine, I could never have known what I wanted done to the bike when it didn't work. I had a lot of help with the engineering side from Bud Aksland, who was my mechanic when I was a junior. Kel always helped too, and we would sit and talk about two strokes and discuss what

Lawson (right) and Gardner are two of the men that Roberts sees as safe bets for any team but he wants to develop his own riders who fit in with his ideas on how the team should operate.

we might try to make the thing go better. We would try ideas, some worked and some turned out to be stupid, but it was all learning.

I'd get into arguments with Kel all the time. I'd want to steepen up the steering head to make it go from left to right faster, and he'd say that was just going to make it wobble. I would be complaining about the wobble, because I didn't think it should do that even with a steep steering head, and yet I was wanting to do something that would only make it worse, that would affect maybe two or three very important corners and would bring my lap time down, but didn't make any sense for the rest of the track.

There was one year when we were racing in America we had production bikes. Yamaha though they would be nice and they sent us over lightweight cranks for the 250s. Kel thought the cranks looked neat and we hoped they would give us an edge. When it came to the first race I rode my butt off and kept shifting the damn thing to try and get some power out of it. Afterwards I said to Kel, 'Are you sure these light cranks work?' and he said, 'Well, the factory say they give more acceleration.' I told him that I didn't think they worked. That was 1974, the year we went to Assen for the Dutch GP; we were taking that motor and I asked to take the old crank as well. So we took two motors, though Kel said that there was no way I was going to be able to keep up in a Grand Prix with a standard heavy crank engine. I tested them back to back and said he could throw the light cranks away, because I could not use them. I had to shift more and the bike dropped its corner speed, so it was harder to get out of the slow speed corners. That was the way things worked out, but if I had not had a certain amount of experience with engines it would have been a pretty hard thing to do, to tell Kel Carruthers, a World Champion, that it wasn't working.

You can be too aware of the motor cycle, to the point that it can adversely affect your riding. You cannot afford to be put off by what might be wrong with the bike once the race has started. Once the flag has dropped I have always tried to win, no matter what was wrong with the bike. There might have been oil all over it, as there was at Silverstone in '79 when the gearbox seal had gone. We won a lot of races when we shouldn't have. You just have to switch off worrying about the bike and get on and ride it.

APPENDICES

KENNY ROBERTS'S
GRAND PRIX STATISTICS
by John Taylor

1978 (500cc)

*Third place for Roberts in the German Grand Prix
– and his first World Championship.*

Gran Premio de Venezuela (San Carlos)
30 laps, 77.08 miles/124.50 km

1	Barry Sheene	Suzuki	95.64 mph/153.92 km/h
2	Pat Hennen	Suzuki	
3	Steve Baker	Suzuki	
RTD	**Kenny Roberts**	**Yamaha**	**Engine**

Grid position   2nd (1m 35.6s)

Gran Premio de Espana (Jarama)
36 laps, 76.15 miles/122.56 km

1	Pat Hennen	Suzuki	79.10 mph/127.30 km/h
2	**Kenny Roberts**	**Yamaha**	
3	Takazumi Katayama	Yamaha	

Grid position   Pole (1m 34.9s)

Grosser Preis von Osterreich (Salzburgring)
35 laps, 92.22 miles/148.42 km

1	**Kenny Roberts**	**Yamaha**	114.08 mph/183.59 km/h
2	Johnny Cecotto	Yamaha	
3	Barry Sheene	Suzuki	

Grid position   2nd (1m 21.87s)

Grand Prix de France (Nogaro)
40 laps, 77.55 miles/124.80 km

1	**Kenny Roberts**	**Yamaha**	82.05 mph/132.04 km/h
2	Pat Hennen	Suzuki	
3	Barry Sheene	Suzuki	

Grid position   3rd (1m 25.48s)

Gran Premio delle Nazioni (Mugello)
28 laps, 91.25 miles /148.64 km

1	**Kenny Roberts**	**Yamaha**	92.36 mph/148.64 km/h
2	Pat Hennen	Suzuki	
3	Marco Lucchinelli	Suzuki	

Grid position   Pole (2m 05.60s)

Grote Prijs van Nederland (Assen)
16 laps, 76.73 miles/123.48 km

1	Johnny Cecotto	Yamaha	95.35 mph/153.45 km/h
2	**Kenny Roberts**	**Yamaha**	
3	Barry Sheene	Suzuki	

Grid position   3rd (3m 03.1s)

Grand Prix de Belgique (Spa)
10 laps, 87.74 miles/141.20 km

1	Wil Hartog	Suzuki	132.14 mph/212.65 km/h
2	**Kenny Roberts**	**Yamaha**	
3	Barry Sheene	Suzuki	

Grid position   5th (3m 51.6s)

Swedish TT (Karlskoga)
40 laps, 78.29 miles/126.00 km

1	Barry Sheene	Suzuki	84.16 mph/135.44 km/h
2	Wil Hartog	Suzuki	
3	Takazumi Katayama	Yamaha	
7	**Kenny Roberts**	**Yamaha**	

Grid position   9th (1m 24.048s)

Finnish Grand Prix (Imatra)
21 laps, 78.68 miles/125.63 km

1	Wil Hartog	Suzuki	103.23 mph/166.13 km/h
2	Takazumi Katayama	Yamaha	
3	Johnny Cecotto	Yamaha	
RTD	**Kenny Roberts**	**Yamaha**	**Ignition**

Grid position   9th (2m 12.1s)

British Grand Prix (Silverstone)
28 laps, 81.96 miles/131.12 km

1	**Kenny Roberts**	**Yamaha**	87.89 mph/141.45 km/h
2	Steve Manship	Suzuki	
3	Barry Sheene	Suzuki	

Grid position   2nd (1m 31.31s)

Grosser Preis von Deutschland (Nürburgring)
6 laps, 85.13 miles/137.01 km

1	Virginio Ferrari	Suzuki	99.45 mph/160.05 km/h
2	Johnny Cecotto	Yamaha	
3	**Kenny Roberts**	**Yamaha**	

Grid position   2nd (8m 32.5s)

Summary
Races 11
1st/4   2nd/3   3rd/1   7th/1   RTD/2

1978 500cc World Championship

1	**Kenny Roberts (USA)**	**Yamaha**	**110 (*4 wins*)**
2	Barry Sheene (GB)	Suzuki	100 (*2 wins*)
3	Johnny Cecotto (YV)	Yamaha	66 (*1 win*)
4	Wil Hartog (NL)	Suzuki	65 (*2 wins*)
5	Takazumi Katayama (J)	Yamaha	53
6	Pat Hennen (USA)	Suzuki	51 (*1 win*)
7	Steve Baker (USA)	Suzuki	42
8	Tepi Länsivuori (SF)	Suzuki	39
9	Marco Lucchinelli (I)	Suzuki	30
10	Michel Rougerie (F)	Suzuki	23

1979 (500cc)

Grosser Preis von Osterreich (Salzburgring)
35 laps, 92.22 miles/148.42 km

1	**Kenny Roberts**	**Yamaha**	114.33 mph/183.99 km/h
2	Virginio Ferrari	Suzuki	
3	Wil Hartog	Suzuki	

Grid position   4th (1m 24.77s)

Grosser Preis von Deutschland (Hockenheim)
19 laps, 80.14 miles/128.98 km

1	Wil Hartog	Suzuki	112.97 mph/181.80 km/h
2	**Kenny Roberts**	**Yamaha**	
3	Virginio Ferrari	Suzuki	

Grid position   5th (2m 17.0s)

Gran Premio delle Nazioni (Imola)
29 laps, 90.83 miles/146.16 km

1	**Kenny Roberts**	**Yamaha**	95.89 mph/154.32 km/h
2	Virginio Ferrari	Suzuki	
3	Tom Herron	Suzuki	

Grid position   2nd (1m 56.18s)

Gran Premio de Espana (Jarama)
36 laps, 76.15 miles/122.56 km

1	**Kenny Roberts**	**Yamaha**	79.91 mph/128.60 km/h
2	Wil Hartog	Suzuki	
3	Mike Baldwin	Suzuki	

Grid position   2nd (1m 34.9s)

Grand Prix de Yougoslavie (Rijeka)
32 laps, 82.88 miles/133.38 km

1	**Kenny Roberts**	**Yamaha**	96.64 mph/155.53 km/h
2	Virginio Ferrari	Suzuki	
3	Franco Uncini	Suzuki	

Grid position   Pole (1m 50.57s)

Grote Prijs van Nederland (Assen)
16 laps, 76.73 miles/123.48 km

1	Virginio Ferrari	Suzuki	97.94 mph/157.63 km/h
2	Barry Sheene	Suzuki	
3	Wil Hartog	Suzuki	
8	**Kenny Roberts**	**Yamaha**	

Grid position   Pole (2m 55.9s)

Swedish TT (Karlskoga)
40 laps, 78.29 miles/126.00 km

1	Barry Sheene	Suzuki	84.89 mph/136.61 km/h
2	Jack Middelburg	Suzuki	
3	Boet van Dulmen	Suzuki	
4	**Kenny Roberts**	**Yamaha**	

Grid position   Pole (1m 21.0s)

Finnish Grand Prix (Imatra)
26 laps, 80.08 miles/128.70 km

1	Boet van Dulmen	Suzuki	91.47 mph/147.20 km/h
2	Randy Mamola	Suzuki	
3	Barry Sheene	Suzuki	
6	**Kenny Roberts**	**Yamaha**	

Grid position   2nd (1m 55.6s)

British Grand Prix (Silverstone)
28 laps, 81.96 miles/131.88 km

1	**Kenny Roberts**	**Yamaha**	114.50 mph/184.27 km/h
2	Barry Sheene	Suzuki	
3	Wil Hartog	Suzuki	

Grid position   Pole (1m 29.81s)

Grand Prix de France (Le Mans)
29 laps, 76.40 miles/153.39 km

1	Barry Sheene	Suzuki	95.31 mph/153.39 km/h
2	Randy Mamola	Suzuki	
3	**Kenny Roberts**	**Yamaha**	

Grid position   Pole (1m 38.13s)

Summary
Races 10
1st/5   2nd/1   3rd/1   4th/1   6th/1   8th/1

1979 500cc World Championship

1	**Kenny Roberts (USA)**	**Yamaha**	**113 (5 wins)**
2	Virginio Ferrari (I)	Suzuki	89 (1 win)
3	Barry Sheene (GB)	Suzuki	87 (3 wins)
4	Wil Hartog (NL)	Suzuki	66 (1 win)
5	Franco Uncini (I)	Suzuki	51
6	Boet van Dulmen (NL)	Suzuki	50 (1 win)
7	Jack Middelburg (NL)	Suzuki	36
8	Randy Mamola (USA)	Suzuki	29
9	Philippe Coulon (F)	Suzuki	29
10	Tom Herron (GB)	Suzuki	28

1980 (500cc)

Roberts leads Lucchinelli, Cecotto, Rossi and van Dulmen at the Dutch TT, 1980.

Gran Premio delle Nazioni (Misano)
40 laps, 86.68 miles/139.52 km

1	**Kenny Roberts**	**Yamaha**	92.89 mph/149.49 km/h
2	Franco Uncini	Suzuki	
3	Graziano Rossi	Suzuki	

Grid position   2nd (1m 22.9s)

Gran Premio de Espana (Jarama)
36 laps, 76.14 miles/122.54 km

1	**Kenny Roberts**	**Yamaha**	79.34 mph/127.69 km/h
2	Marco Lucchinelli	Suzuki	
3	Randy Mamola	Suzuki	

Grid position   Pole (1m 31.79s)

Grand Prix de France (Paul Ricard)
21 laps, 75.81 miles/122.01 km

1	**Kenny Roberts**	**Yamaha**	102.84 mph/165.50 km/h
2	Randy Mamola	Suzuki	
3	Marco Lucchinelli	Suzuki	

Grid position   2nd (2m 05.33s)

Grote Prijs van Nederland (Assen)
16 laps, 76.73 miles/123.48 km

1	Jack Middelburg	Yamaha	95.19 mph/153.19 km/h
2	Graziano Rossi	Suzuki	
3	Franco Uncini	Suzuki	
RTD	**Kenny Roberts**	**Yamaha**	**Tyres**

Grid position   5th (2m 58.9s)

Grand Prix de Belgique (Zolder)
30 laps, 79.44 miles/127.86 km

1	Randy Mamola	Suzuki	93.25 mph/150.07 km/h
2	Marco Lucchinelli	Suzuki	
3	**Kenny Roberts**	**Yamaha**	

Grid position   6th (1m 42.26s)

Finnish Grand Prix (Imatra)
26 laps, 80.08 miles/128.70 km

1	Wil Hartog	Suzuki	94.27 mph/151.71 km/h
2	**Kenny Roberts**	**Yamaha**	
3	Franco Uncini	Suzuki	

Grid position   5th (1m 56.1s)

British Grand Prix (Silverstone)
28 laps, 81.96 miles/131.88 km

1	Randy Mamola	Suzuki	114.68 mph/184.56 km/h
2	**Kenny Roberts**	**Yamaha**	
3	Marco Lucchinelli	Suzuki	

Grid position   Pole (1m 30.71s)

Grosser Preis von Deutschland (Nürburgring)
6 laps, 85.13 miles/137.01 km

1	Marco Lucchinelli	Suzuki	100.88 mph/162.35 km/h
2	Graeme Crosby	Suzuki	
3	Wil Hartog	Suzuki	
4	**Kenny Roberts**	**Yamaha**	

Grid position   2nd (8m 27.20s)

Summary
Races 8
1st/3 2nd/2 3rd/1 4th/1 RTD/1

1980 500cc World Championship

1	**Kenny Roberts (USA)**	**Yamaha**	**87** (*3 wins*)
2	Randy Mamola (USA)	Suzuki	72 (*2 wins*)
3	Marco Lucchinelli (I)	Suzuki	59 (*1 win*)
4	Franco Uncini (I)	Suzuki	50
5	Graziano Rossi (I)	Suzuki	38
6=	Johnny Cecotto (YV)	Yamaha	31
6=	Wil Hartog (NL)	Suzuki	31 (*1 win*)
8	Graeme Crosby (NZ)	Suzuki	29
9	Jack Middelburg (NL)	Yamaha	20 (*1 win*)
10	Takazumi Katayama (J)	Suzuki	18

1981 (500cc)

Grosser Preis von Osterreich (Salzburgring)

35 laps, 92.22 miles/148.42 km

1	Randy Mamola	Suzuki	114.91 mph/184.93 km/h
2	Graeme Crosby	Suzuki	
3	Hiroyuki Kawasaki	Suzuki	
RTD	**Kenny Roberts**	**Yamaha**	**Rear suspension**

Grid position   Not in top ten/practice accident

Grosser Preis von Deutschland (Hockenheim)

19 laps, 80.14 miles/128.99 km

1	**Kenny Roberts**	**Yamaha**	114.22 mph/183.82 km/h
2	Randy Mamola	Suzuki	
3	Marco Lucchinelli	Suzuki	

Grid position   3rd (2m 13.67s)

Gran Premio delle Nazioni (Monza)

24 laps, 86.50 miles/139.20 km

1	**Kenny Roberts**	**Yamaha**	99.67 mph/160.40 km/h
2	Graeme Crosby	Suzuki	
3	Barry Sheene	Yamaha	

Grid position   3rd (1m 54.08s)

Grand Prix de France (Paul Ricard)

21 laps, 75.81 miles/122.01 km

1	Marco Lucchinelli	Suzuki	102.94 mph/165.67 km/h
2	Randy Mamola	Suzuki	
3	Graeme Crosby	Suzuki	
5	**Kenny Roberts**	**Yamaha**	

Grid position   2nd (2m 04.74s)

Grand Prix de Yougoslavie (Rijeka)

32 laps, 82.88 miles/133.38 km

1	Randy Mamola	Suzuki	97.72 mph/157.26 km/h
2	Marco Lucchinelli	Suzuki	
3	**Kenny Roberts**	**Yamaha**	

Grid position   2nd (1m 34.6s)

Grote Prijs van Nederland (Assen)

16 laps, 76.40 miles/122.96 km

1	Marco Lucchinelli	Suzuki	91.19 mph/146.76 km/h
2	Boet van Dulmen	Yamaha	
3	Kork Ballington	Kawasaki	
DNS	**Kenny Roberts**	**Yamaha**	**Brake pad welded to disc**

Grid position   2nd (2m 51.9s)

Grand Prix de Belgique (Spa)

20 laps, 86.64 miles/139.44 km

1	Marco Lucchinelli	Suzuki	95.40 mph/153.53 km/h
2	**Kenny Roberts**	**Yamaha**	
3	Randy Mamola	Yamaha	

Grid position   3rd (2m 39.96s)

Gran Premio di San Marino (Imola)

21 laps, 65.77 miles/105.84 km

1	Marco Lucchinelli	Suzuki	93.21 mph/150.01 km/h
2	Barry Sheene	Yamaha	
3	Graeme Crosby	Suzuki	
DNS	**Kenny Roberts**	**Yamaha**	**Unwell**

Grid position   2nd (1m 57.20s)

British Grand Prix (Silverstone)

28 laps, 81.96 miles/131.91 km

1	Jack Middelburg	Suzuki	113.29 mph/183.32 km/h
2	**Kenny Roberts**	**Yamaha**	
3	Randy Mamola	Suzuki	

Grid position   4th (1m 31.13s)

Finnish Grand Prix (Imatra)

25 laps, 77.00 miles/123.75 km

1	Marco Lucchinelli	Suzuki	95.94 mph/154.40 km/h
2	Randy Mamola	Suzuki	
3	Kork Ballington	Kawasaki	
7	**Kenny Roberts**	**Yamaha**	

Grid position   8th (1m 55.9s)

Swedish TT (Anderstorp)

30 laps, 74.91 miles/120.54 km

1	Barry Sheene	Yamaha	87.32 mph/140.53 km/h
2	Boet van Dulmen	Yamaha	
3	Jack Middelburg	Suzuki	
RTD	**Kenny Roberts**	**Yamaha**	**Tyres**

Grid position   3rd (1m 40.70s)

Summary

Races 9
1st/2 2nd/2 3rd/1 5th/1 7th/1 RTD/2

Holding off the Suzukis of Lucchinelli and Sheene,
1981 French Grand Prix.

1981 500cc World Championship

1	Marco Lucchinelli (I)	Suzuki	105 (*5 wins*)
2	Randy Mamola (USA)	Suzuki	94 (*2 wins*)
3	**Kenny Roberts (USA)**	**Yamaha**	**74 (*2 wins*)**
4	Barry Sheene (GB)	Yamaha	72 (*1 win*)
5	Graeme Crosby (NZ)	Suzuki	68
6	Boet van Dulmen (NL)	Yamaha	64
7	Jack Middelburg (NL)	Suzuki	60 (*1 win*)
8	Kork Ballington (ZA)	Kawasaki	43
9	Marc Fontan (F)	Yamaha	25
10	Hiroyuki Kawasaki (J)	Suzuki	19

1982 500cc World Championship

1	Franco Uncini (I)	Suzuki	103 (*5 wins*)
2	Graeme Crosby (NZ)	Yamaha	76
3	Freddie Spencer (USA)	Honda	72 (*2 wins*)
4=	**Kenny Roberts (USA)**	**Yamaha**	**68** (*2 wins*)
4=	Barry Sheene (GB)	Yamaha	68
6	Randy Mamola (USA)	Suzuki	65 (*1 win*)
7	Takazumi Katayama (J)	Honda	48 (*1 win*)
8	Marco Lucchinelli (I)	Honda	43
9	Kork Ballington (ZA)	Kawasaki	31
10	Marc Fontan (F)	Yamaha	29

1982 (500cc)

Gran Premio de la Republica Argentina (Buenos Aires)

32 laps, 79.23 miles/127.49 km

1	**Kenny Roberts**	**Yamaha**	93.66 mph/150.73 km/h
2	Barry Sheene	Yamaha	
3	Freddie Spencer	Honda	

Grid position   Pole (1m 34.05s)

Grosser Preis von Osterreich (Salzburgring)

29 laps, 76.41 miles/122.97 km

1	Franco Uncini	Suzuki	115.26 mph/185.50 km/h
2	Barry Sheene	Yamaha	
3	**Kenny Roberts**	**Yamaha**	

Grid position   3rd (1m 26.45s)

Gran Premio de Espana (Jarama)

37 laps, 76.15 miles/122.54 km

1	**Kenny Roberts**	**Yamaha**	79.97 mph/128.70 km/h
2	Barry Sheene	Yamaha	
3	Franco Uncini	Suzuki	

Grid position   2nd (1m 31.27s)

Gran Premio delle Nazioni (Misano)

40 laps, 86.68 miles/139.52 km

1	Franco Uncini	Suzuki	93.74 mph/150.86 km/h
2	Freddie Spencer	Honda	
3	Graeme Crosby	Yamaha	
4	**Kenny Roberts**	**Yamaha**	

Grid position   5th (1m 22.62s)

Grote Prijs van Nederland (Assen)

16 laps, 76.40 miles/122.94 km

1	Franco Uncini	Suzuki	98.78 mph/158.97 km/h
2	**Kenny Roberts**	**Yamaha**	
3	Barry Sheene	Yamaha	

Grid position   Pole (2m 49.87s)

Grand Prix de Belgique (Spa)

20 laps, 86.64 miles/139.44 km

1	Freddie Spencer	Honda	98.15 mph/157.96 km/h
2	Barry Sheene	Yamaha	
3	Franco Uncini	Suzuki	
4	**Kenny Roberts**	**Yamaha**	

Grid position   5th (2m 40.212s)

Grand Prix de Yougoslavie (Rijeka)

32 laps, 82.88 miles/133.38 km

1	Franco Uncini	Suzuki	98.41 mph/158.38 km/h
2	Graeme Crosby	Yamaha	
3	Barry Sheene	Yamaha	
RTD	**Kenny Roberts**	**Yamaha**	Ignition

Grid position   6th (1m 34.18s)

British Grand Prix (Silverstone)

28 laps, 81.96 miles/131.91 km

1	Franco Uncini	Suzuki	114.62 mph/184.46 km/h
2	Freddie Spencer	Honda	
3	Graeme Crosby	Yamaha	
RTD	**Kenny Roberts**	**Yamaha**	Crashed

Grid position   Pole (1m 29.84s)

Note: Roberts took no part in the Swedish, San Marino and German Grands Prix because of the knee and finger injuries he suffered at Silverstone.

Summary
Races 8
1st/2   2nd/1   3rd/1   4th/2   RTD/2

1983 (500cc)

*Roberts leads Spencer during practice at Kyalami
in '83. The V four refused to start well and while
Spencer romped away, Roberts had to fight
through to second.*

1983 500cc World Championship

1	Freddie Spencer (USA)	Honda	144 (*6 wins*)
2	**Kenny Roberts (USA)**	**Yamaha**	**142** (*6 wins*)
3	Randy Mamola (USA)	Suzuki	89
4	Eddie Lawson (USA)	Yamaha	78
5	Takazumi Katayama (J)	Honda	77
6	Marc Fontan (F)	Yamaha	64
7	Marco Lucchinelli (I)	Honda	48
8=	Ron Haslam (GB)	Honda	31
8=	Franco Uncini (I)	Suzuki	31
10	Raymond Roche (F)	Honda	22

South African Grand Prix (Kyalami)

30 laps, 76.50 miles/123.12 km

1	Freddie Spencer	Honda	104.37 mph/167.97 km/h
2	**Kenny Roberts**	**Yamaha**	
3	Ron Haslam	Honda	

Grid position   4th (1m 26.94s)

Grand Prix de France (Le Mans)

29 laps, 76.42 miles/122.96 km

1	Freddie Spencer	Honda	95.91 mph/154.35 km/h
2	Marco Lucchinelli	Honda	
3	Ron Haslam	Honda	
4	**Kenny Roberts**	**Yamaha**	

Grid position   Pole (1m 36.80s)

Gran Premio delle Nazioni (Monza)

24 laps, 86.50 miles/139.20 km

1	Freddie Spencer	Honda	113.38 mph/182.47 km/h
2	Randy Mamola	Suzuki	
3	Eddie Lawson	Yamaha	
RTD	**Kenny Roberts**	**Yamaha**	**Out of fuel**

Grid position   Pole (1m 52.69s)

Grosser Preis von Deutschland (Hockenheim)

15 laps, 63.27 miles/101.84 km

1	**Kenny Roberts**	**Yamaha**	115.16 mph/185.33 km/h
2	Takazumi Katayama	Honda	
3	Marco Lucchinelli	Honda	

Grid position   2nd (2m 10.25s)

Gran Premio de Espana (Jarama)

37 laps, 76.15 miles/122.54 km

1	Freddie Spencer	Honda	81.16 mph/130.62 km/h
2	**Kenny Roberts**	**Yamaha**	
3	Takazumi Katayama	Honda	

Grid position   2nd (1m 30.37s)

Grosser Preis von Osterreich (Salzburgring)

31 laps, 81.68 miles/131.46 km

1	**Kenny Roberts**	**Yamaha**	118.25 mph/190.30 km/h
2	Eddie Lawson	Yamaha	
3	Randy Mamola	Suzuki	

Grid position   Pole (1m 17.89s)

Grand Prix de Yougoslavie (Rijeka)

32 laps, 82.88 miles/133.38 km

1	Freddie Spencer	Honda	98.82 mph/159.03 km/h
2	Randy Mamola	Suzuki	
3	Eddie Lawson	Yamaha	
4	**Kenny Roberts**	**Yamaha**	

Grid position   2nd (1m 32.562s)

Grote Prijs van Nederland (Assen)

16 laps, 76.40 miles/122.94 km

1	**Kenny Roberts**	**Yamaha**	100.79 mph/162.20 km/h
2	Takazumi Katayama	Honda	
3	Freddie Spencer	Honda	

Grid position   Pole (2m 48.52s)

Grand Prix de Belgique (Spa)

20 laps, 86.28 miles/138.84 km

1	**Kenny Roberts**	**Yamaha**	100.81 mph/162.23 km/h
2	Freddie Spencer	Honda	
3	Randy Mamola	Suzuki	

Grid position   2nd (2m 32.79s)

British Grand Prix (Silverstone)

28 laps, 81.96 miles/131.91 km

1	**Kenny Roberts**	**Yamaha**	116.20 mph/187.01 km/h
2	Freddie Spencer	Honda	
3	Randy Mamola	Suzuki	

Grid position   Pole (1m 28.00s)

Swedish TT (Anderstorp)

30 laps, 75.15 miles/120.93 km

1	Freddie Spencer	Honda	91.46 mph/147.19 km/h
2	**Kenny Roberts**	**Yamaha**	
3	Takazumi Katayama	Honda	

Grid position   2nd (1m 38.81s)

Gran Premio di San Marino (Imola)

25 laps, 78.30 miles/126.00 km

1	**Kenny Roberts**	**Yamaha**	97.31 mph/156.60 km/h
2	Freddie Spencer	Honda	
3	Eddie Lawson	Yamaha	

Grid position   Pole (1m 53.49s)

Summary

Races 12
1st/6   2nd/3   4th/2   RTD/1

Engine problems destroyed Roberts's chances of
winning the 250cc Championship in 1978.

1974 (250cc)

Grote Prijs van Nederland (Assen)
16 laps, 76.59 miles/123.26 km

1	Walter Villa	Harley-Davidson	91.21 mph/146.97 km/h
2	Bruno Kneubühler	Yamaha	
3	**Kenny Roberts**	**Yamaha**	

Grid position   Pole (3m 09.5s)

1978 (250cc)

Gran Premio de Venezuela (San Carlos)
28 laps, 71.94 miles/115.78 km

1	**Kenny Roberts**	**Yamaha**	91.34 mph/146.99 km/h
2	Carlos Lavado	Yamaha	
3	Patrick Fernandez	Yamaha	

Grid position   2nd (1m 39.4s)

Gran Premio de Espana (Jarama)
30 laps, 63.46 miles/102.13 km

1	Gregg Hansford	Kawasaki	76.99 mph/123.91 km/h
2	**Kenny Roberts**	**Yamaha**	
3	Franco Uncini	Yamaha	

Grid position   Pole (1m 38.7s)

Grand Prix de France (Nogaro)
33 laps, 63.98 miles/102.96 km

1	Gregg Hansford	Kawasaki	79.36 mph/127.72 km/h
2	**Kenny Roberts**	**Yamaha**	
3	Kork Ballington	Kawasaki	

Grid position   7th (1m 29.76s)

Gran Premio delle Nazioni (Mugello)
23 laps, 74.96 miles/120.64 km

1	Kork Ballington	Kawasaki	89.26 mph/143.64 km/h
2	Gregg Hansford	Kawasaki	
3	Franco Uncini	Yamaha	
RTD	**Kenny Roberts**	**Yamaha**	**Engine**

Grid position   Pole (2m 11.36s)

Grote Prijs van Nederland (Assen)
15 laps, 71.93 miles/115.77 km

1	**Kenny Roberts**	**Yamaha**	87.18 mph/140.31 km/h
2	Kork Ballington	Kawasaki	
3	Gregg Hansford	Kawasaki	

Grid position   Pole (3m 09.0s)

Grand Prix de Belgique (Spa)
9 laps, 78.96 miles/127.08 km

1	Paolo Pileri	Morbidelli	116.74 mph/187.88 km/h
2	Franco Uncini	Yamaha	
3	Walter Villa	Harley-Davidson	
RTD	**Kenny Roberts**	**Yamaha**	**Engine**

Grid position   7th (4m 14.5s)

Finnish Grand Prix (Imatra)
19 laps, 71.19 miles/114.57 km

1	Kork Ballington	Kawasaki	97.27 mph/156.44 km/h
2	Gregg Hansford	Kawasaki	
3	Mario Lega	Morbidelli	
RTD	**Kenny Roberts**	**Yamaha**	**Misfire**

Grid position   4th (2m 20.2s)

British Grand Prix (Silverstone)
26 laps, 76.10 miles/121.76 km

1	Anton Mang	Kawasaki	106.05 mph/170.67 km/h
2	Tom Herron	Yamaha	
3	Raymond Roche	Yamaha	
RTD	**Kenny Roberts**	**Yamaha**	**Engine**

Grid position   2nd (1m 37.52s)

Grosser Preis von Deutschland (Nürburgring)
5 laps, 70.94 miles/114.18 km

1	Kork Ballington	Kawasaki	95.25 mph/153.29 km/h
2	Gregg Hansford	Kawasaki	
3	Tom Herron	Yamaha	
RTD	**Kenny Roberts**	**Yamaha**	**Engine**

Grid position   5th (9m 08.3s)

Summary
Races 9
1st/2   2nd/2   RTD/5

1978 250cc World Championship

1	Kork Ballington (ZA)	Kawasaki	124 (*4 wins*)
2	Gregg Hansford (AUS)	Kawasaki	118 (*4 wins*)
3	Patrick Fernandez (F)	Yamaha	55
4	**Kenny Roberts (USA)**	**Yamaha**	**54** (*2 wins*)
5	Anton Mang (D)	Kawasaki	52 (*1 win*)
6	Tom Herron (GB)	Yamaha	48
7	Mario Lega (I)	Morbidelli	44
8	Franco Uncini (I)	Yamaha	42
9	Jon Ekerold (ZA)	Yamaha/Morbidelli	40
10	Paolo Pileri (I)	Morbidelli	35 (*1 win*)

Second to Spencer in the Championship but still
'King Kenny' to many: Roberts on the rostrum with
Spencer and Lawson after the San Marino Grand
Prix at Imola in 1983.

Summary 1978 – 1983 (500cc)

Year	1978	1979	1980	1981	1982	1983	Total
Races	11	10	8	9	8	12	58
Points	110	113	87	74	68	142	594
1st	4	5	3	2	2	6	22
2nd	3	1	2	2	1	3	12
3rd	1	1	1	1	1	–	5
4th	–	1	1	–	2	2	6
5th	–	–	–	1	–	–	1
6th	–	1	–	–	–	–	1
7th	1	–	–	1	–	–	2
8th	–	1	–	–	–	–	1
RTD	2	–	1	2	2	1	8

Summary 1974 and 1978 (250cc)

Class 250
Races 10
Points 64
1st/2 2nd/2 3rd/1 RTD/5

500cc TECHNICAL SPECIFICATIONS

Kenny Roberts's 500cc Grand Prix career spanned the six seasons
from 1978 to 1983. These are the specifications of the machines he
rode, together with the 1977 OW35 raced by Steve Baker and
referred to by Roberts in the text and the 1984 OW76 which
Eddie Lawson used to win the World Championship and which
Roberts rode at the Anglo-American Match Races that year.

*Kel Carruthers takes charge
of Roberts's 1979 OW45.*

1977 OW35

Engine: 54mm x 54mm, water-cooled, transverse four-cylinder two stroke; piston-ported induction; one plain piston ring; dry clutch with six friction and seven steel plates, six springs. *Gearbox*: six-speed; drum selection. *Carburettors*: cylindrical-slide Mikuni.
Frame: Yamaha twin-loop steel tube cradle, taper roller head bearings; tubular steel triangulated swing arm; cantilever monoshock rear suspension, one Yamaha unit, coil-spring, oil damping; Yamaha forks, coil-springs, oil-damped. *Wheels*: Morris. *Tyres*: Goodyear. *Brakes*: two Yamaha steel discs at front and a single Yamaha at rear; Yamaha pads. *Plugs*: Champion. *Gearbox and engine oil*: Bel-ray.

1978 OW35

Engine: 56mm x 50.5mm, water-cooled, transverse four-cylinder two stroke; piston-ported induction; cylindrical exhaust valve; one piston ring; dry clutch with six friction and seven steel plates, six springs. *Gearbox*: six-speed; drum selection. *Carburettors*: cylindrical-slide Mikuni.
Frame: Yamaha twin-loop steel tube cradle, taper roller head bearings; aluminium rectangular-section tube swing arm; cantilever monoshock rear suspension, one Yamaha unit, coil-spring, oil damping; Yamaha forks, coil-springs, oil-damped. *Wheels*: Morris. *Tyres*: Goodyear. *Brakes*: two Yamaha steel discs at front and a single Yamaha at rear. Yamaha calipers front and rear. Yamaha pads. *Plugs*: Champion. *Gearbox and engine oil*: Bel-Ray.

1979 OW45

Engine: 56mm x 50.6mm, water-cooled, transverse four-cylinder two stroke; piston-ported induction; four transfer and one exhaust ports (electronically-controlled cylindrical exhaust valve); one plain piston ring; two pressed cranks, four roller bearings each; dry clutch with seven friction and eight steel plates, six springs. *Gearbox*: six-speed; drum selection. *Carburettors*: Mikuni or Lectron.
Frame: Yamaha twin-loop steel tube cradle, taper roller head bearings; rectangular-section tubular aluminium swing arm, needle roller bearings; cantilever monoshock rear suspension, one Yamaha unit, coil-spring plus nitrogen pressure, oil damping, adjustable; Yamaha forks, coil-springs, oil-damped, adjustable. *Wheels*: Morris. *Tyres*: Goodyear. *Brakes*: two Yamaha steel discs at front (320mm) and a single Yamaha at rear (220mm); Brembo aluminium calipers front, Nissin rear, Yamaha pads. *Plugs*: Champion. *Gearbox and engine oil*: Bel-Ray.

1980 OW48

The familiar transverse four (below) with power-jet carburettors and the single monoshock unit that Roberts hated so much. Later in 1980, a square-section aluminium frame became available (below right) and at the Dutch TT at Assen the team wheeled out a variation with the outer cylinders reversed to provide a better run for the exhaust system. The OW48 had guillotine instead of cylindrical exhaust valves and a choice of carburettors. Some were aluminium and some magnesium. Three sizes were used, 34mm, 36mm and 38mm, either flat-slided or cylindrical. The flat-slide carbs proved best for fast circuits, while the smaller diameter, cylindrical carbs gave more torque on tighter, twisty tracks.

Engine: 56mm x 50.6mm, water-cooled, transverse four-cylinder two stroke; piston-ported induction; four transfer and one exhaust ports (electronically-controlled guillotine exhaust valve); one plain piston ring; roller big ends and needle roller small ends; two pressed cranks, four roller bearings each; dry clutch with seven friction and seven steel plates, six springs. *Gearbox:* six-speed with four possible ratios for 1st and 2nd, and three for 3rd and 4th; drum selection. *Carburettors:* 34, 36 or 38mm cylindrical- or flat-slide Mikuni.

Frame: Yamaha twin-loop square-section aluminium tube cradle, taper roller head bearings; square-section aluminium swing arm, needle roller bearings; cantilever monoshock rear suspension, one Yamaha unit, coil-spring plus 20kg nitrogen pressure, oil damping, adjustable for both compression and rebound; Kyaba forks, coil-springs plus 0.7 to 1.4kg air pressure, oil-damped, adjustable by changing internal jets (alternative non-adjustable damping forks had brakeline-pressure-activated anti-dive damping constriction). *Wheels:* Morris, commonly used sizes 2.50in. x 18in. front and 3.50in. or 4.00in. x 17in. rear. *Tyres:* Goodyear. *Brakes:* two Yamaha steel discs at front (320mm) and a single Yamaha at rear (220mm); Yamaha aluminium calipers front and rear, Yamaha pads. *Plugs:* Champion N84G. *Gearbox and engine oil:* Bel-Ray.

(Outer cylinders reversed from the Dutch TT onwards; called the OW48R when the cylindrical exhaust valves used previously were also replaced by the guillotine valves.)

Below left: The reverse-cylinder version of the 1980 OW48. The frame was made from square-section tubing but double tubes were used along the top runs for extra strength. The frame was painted black to disguise the fact that it was aluminium.

Below right: One of the front fork arrangements available to Roberts during the 1980 season. This featured a brake-fluid-pressure-activated anti-dive system but more popular was the fork with no anti-dive but external oil lines where the damping jets could be quickly changed. Roberts has never favoured anti-dive systems but rather a reliable and easily adjustable spring and damping arrangement.

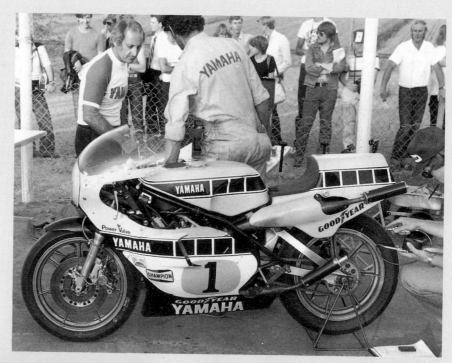

1981 OW54

Engine: 56mm x 50.6mm, water-cooled, square four-cylinder two stroke; disc-valve induction; five transfer and one exhaust ports (electronically-controlled guillotine exhaust valve); one plain piston-ring; roller big ends and needle roller small ends; four pressed cranks, two roller bearings each; dry clutch with five friction and six steel plates, six springs. *Gearbox*: six-speed, alternative ratios for all gears; drum selection. *Carburettors*: 34 or 36mm cylindrical-slide Mikuni.

Frame: Yamaha twin-loop square-section aluminium tube cradle, taper roller head bearings; rectangular-section aluminium swing arm, needle roller bearings; cantilever monoshock rear suspension, one Yamaha unit, coil-spring plus 18kg nitrogen pressure, oil damping, adjustable. Yamaha forks, coil-spring plus air pressure, oil-damped, adjustable. *Wheels*: Morris, commonly used sizes 2.60in. x 16in. front and 4.50in. x 18in. rear. *Tyres*: Goodyear. *Brakes*: two Yamaha steel discs at front (320mm) and a single Yamaha at rear (220mm); Yamaha aluminium calipers front and rear, Yamaha pads. *Plugs*: Champion N54G. *Gearbox and engine oil*: Bel-Ray.

The 1981 OW54 Yamaha in the pit road at Silverstone. Aluminium had replaced steel as the frame material but the tube section had not increased and there was no way that this could cope with the power of the square four. The rear suspension was just a variation on the old monoshock theme and although several ideas were tried through the year, nothing worked so that, with the engine characteristics and the Goodyear tyres to consider as well, Roberts had his hands full trying to work out which was the greatest villain.

1982 OW61

Engine: 56mm x 50.6mm, water-cooled, V four-cylinder two stroke; disc-valve induction; five transfer and one exhaust ports (electronically-controlled guillotine exhaust valve); one plain piston ring; roller big ends and needle roller small ends; pressed cranks, four roller bearings each; dry clutch with five friction and six steel plates, six springs. *Gearbox*: six-speed, alternative ratios for all gears; drum selection. *Carburettors*: 34 or 36mm cylindrical-or flat-slide Mikuni.

Frame: Yamaha twin-spar rectangular- and square-section aluminium tube cradle, taper roller head bearings; rectangular- and square-section tubular aluminium swing arm, needle roller bearings; rocker arm rear suspension with single Yamaha unit compressed from both ends, coil-spring plus 10kg nitrogen pressure, oil damping, adjustable; Yamaha forks, coil-springs, oil-damped, adjustable. *Wheels*: Morris, commonly used sizes 3.00in. x 16in. front and 5.00in. x 18in. rear. *Tyres*: Dunlop. *Brakes*: two Yamaha steel discs at front (300mm) and a single Yamaha at rear (220mm); Yamaha aluminium calipers front and rear, Yamaha pads. *Plugs*: Champion N84G. *Gearbox and engine oil*: Castrol.

1983 OW70

Engine: 56mm x 50.6mm, water-cooled, V four-cylinder two stroke; disc-valve induction; five transfer and one exhaust ports (electronically-controlled guillotine exhaust valve); one plain piston ring; roller big ends and needle roller small ends; two pressed cranks, four roller bearings each; dry clutch with five friction and six steel plates, six springs. *Gearbox*: six-speed, alternative ratios for all gears; drum selection. *Carburettors*: 34mm flat-slide Mikuni.

Frame: Yamaha twin-spar fabricated box-section aluminium, taper roller head bearings; box-section aluminium swing arm, needle roller bearings; lower end-linked rear suspension, one Ohlins unit, coil-spring plus 10kg nitrogen pressure, oil damping, adjustable; Yamaha forks, coil-springs, oil-damped, adjustable. *Wheels*: Morris, commonly used sizes 2.75 in. x 18in. or 3.00in. x 16in. front and 5.00in. x 18in. rear. *Tyres*: Dunlop. *Brakes*: two Brembo steel discs at front (300mm) and a single Yamaha at rear (220mm); Brembo aluminium calipers front and rear, Brembo pads. *Plugs*: Champion N84. *Gearbox and engine oil*: Castrol.

1984 OW76

Engine: 56mm x 50.6mm, water-cooled, V four-cylinder two stroke; crankcase reed-valve induction; five transfer and one exhaust ports (electronically-controlled guillotine exhaust valve); one plain piston ring; roller big ends and needle roller small ends; two pressed cranks, four roller bearings each; dry clutch with five friction and six steel plates, six springs. *Gearbox*: six-speed, alternative ratios for all gears; drum selection. *Carburettors*: 34 or 35mm flat-slide Mikuni.

Frame: Yamaha twin-spar fabricated box-section aluminium, taper roller head bearings; box-section aluminium swing arm, needle roller bearings; lower end-linked rear suspension, one Ohlins unit, coil-spring plus nitrogen pressure, oil damping, adjustable; Yamaha forks, coil-springs, oil-damped, adjustable. *Wheels*: Campagnolo, commonly used sizes 3.00in. x 17in. front and 4.00in. or 4.50in. x 18in. rear. *Tyres*: Dunlop. *Brakes*: two Brembo cast-steel discs at front (320mm) and a single Brembo at rear (220mm); Brembo aluminium calipers front and rear, Brembo pads. *Plugs*: NGK. *Gearbox and engine oil*: Castrol.

The 1983 OW70 Yamaha featured a mechanically-operated anti-dive system (left) and a finned reservoir on the front of the fork. Movement of the caliper blocked off damping holes inside the fork but the system was usually adjusted to zero.

Right: The 1983 OW70 Yamaha, the second of the V fours: like the first it used disc-valve induction. The two discs rotated flat on the crankcases between the cylinder banks. The engine was a bad starter but what pleased Roberts more than anything was the use of the Öhlins rear suspension unit.

Right: The lower cylinders and extra radiator of the 1983 OW70 Yamaha show beneath the main rad. It was such a maze of frame tubes and plumbing that the mechanics hated it. The twin-spar frame was developing and over later seasons would become bigger and bigger with gains in stiffness.

Index

Numbers in italics refer to illustrations or captions